THE EPIC OF EDEN

Psalms

EXPERIENCE THE BOOK THAT SPEAKS FOR US

T0243966

EIGHT-SESSION BIBLE STUDY GUIDE

SANDRA L. RICHTER

HarperChristian Resources

Contents

Acknowledgments

As always, this *Epic of Eden* study of the book of Psalms is dedicated to all the students with whom I have had the privilege of learning this material. The Psalms are a gift to the church, and studying them has been a gift to me. May this deep dive into their content bring about joy, comfort, and a vision for the Almighty not glimpsed before!

This project could not have been completed without the colossal investment of many people. My deepest gratitude to Sara Riemersma, acquisitions editor and general mastermind of Zondervan/HarperChrisitian Resources, for her enthusiastic vision and masterful coordination of this project. Sara's tireless editing of video, text, and content is matched only by her commitment to excellence. My thanks as well to John Raymond for his behind-the-scenes leadership and "pinch-hitting" when we were in a pinch. To Marshall McLaughlin and his team from ProcessCreative, for hours (and hours) of filming under very challenging COVID conditions, as well as super creative ideas and editing that made all things beautiful. To Dale Williams, our visual editor, who tracked down countless images to best represent the material. And to Jessie Steffes for her dedicated work with our graphics and slides. To Kathy Noftsinger, my long-journey colaborer in the Epic dream. Kathy's dedication to these projects, as they morph from vision to video, is a constant source of strength, insight, and encouragement to me, and I am deeply grateful. Last but not least, to my beloved Steven, Noël, and Elise, who have paid the price of too many late nights and weekends away in order to bring this curriculum to its current state, my forever thanks. And to every pastor and lay leader who diligently sets about the task of teaching the people of God about their God, our team is grateful to say that the *Epic of Eden: Psalms* is here. Let the adventure begin!

Schedule to Follow

SESSION 1

GROUP MEETING
- Distribute study guides
- Watch Video Session 1—The Hymnbook of Ancient Israel
  Use Streaming Video code on inside front cover or DVD

INDIVIDUAL STUDY
- The Hymnbook of Ancient Israel
- Who Wrote the Psalms & Why?

This content will cover both Video Sessions 1 and 2

SESSION 2

GROUP MEETING
- Watch Video Session 2—Who Wrote the Psalms & Why?
  Use Streaming Video code on inside front cover or DVD
- Discuss homework and video teaching

INDIVIDUAL STUDY
- Interpreting the Psalms: Sacred Space

SESSION 3

GROUP MEETING

- Watch Video Session 3—Interpreting the Psalms: Sacred Space
  Use Streaming Video code on inside front cover or DVD
- Discuss homework and video teaching

INDIVIDUAL STUDY

- Interpreting the Psalms: Theocracy

SESSION 4

GROUP MEETING

- Watch Video Session 4—Interpreting the Psalms: Theocracy
  Use Streaming Video code on inside front cover or DVD
- Discuss homework and video teaching

INDIVIDUAL STUDY

- The Power of Poetry

SESSION 5

GROUP MEETING

- Watch Video Session 5—The Power of Poetry
  Use Streaming Video code on inside front cover or DVD
- Discuss homework and video teaching

INDIVIDUAL STUDY

- Lord, Like a Shepherd Lead Us

SESSION 6

GROUP MEETING

- Watch Video Session 6—Lord, Like a Shepherd Lead Us
  Use Streaming Video code on inside front cover or DVD
- Discuss homework and video teaching

INDIVIDUAL STUDY

- Anatomy of a Lament

SESSION 7

GROUP MEETING

- Watch Video Session 7—Anatomy of a Lament
  Use Streaming Video code on inside front cover or DVD
- Discuss homework and video teaching

INDIVIDUAL STUDY

- Jesus and the Psalms

SESSION 8

FINAL GROUP MEETING

- Watch Video Session 8: Jesus and the Psalms
- Discuss homework, video teaching, and the study overall

How Is This Going to Work?

If your group has tackled an *Epic of Eden* study before, you're already pros. If not, here's the plan:

○ The Bible study revolves around a set of eight filmed teaching sessions with me, Dr. Sandy Richter. Each study guide has streaming video access instructions printed on the inside cover. With this access, you can view the videos from any device. If you prefer, DVD is available for purchase.

○ The second component is this study guide, which contains four lessons to be done independently at home before you watch the next video teaching. The first three lessons focus on the upcoming week's video teaching.

○ The fourth lesson is a "bonus psalm!" Do as much or as little individual study as your schedule permits. No pressure, really.

○ The study guide is designed so that the homework will (ideally) be completed before watching the videos—except for session one!

○ Once per week your group will gather to view the video teaching, talk about the individual work from the week, and engage in group discussion about the video. Again, video is available either streaming, using the access instructions on the inside cover, or on DVD.

You may want to plan a little extra time for your first gathering as you meet each other, get your books, drink some coffee, have some snacks (a must for every gathering, really), and dive into the first video. (The first video includes an introduction to the larger study as well as the first lesson.)

Introduction to the Book of Psalms

Enthroned upon the Tehilim (תהלים) of Israel

Psalms is perhaps the most beloved book of our Bibles. This anthology of prayers and praises is so familiar to us that quotations find their way onto dedicatory plaques and national monuments, songs and movie scripts, even the scenic overlooks at the Grand Canyon.[1] Indeed, the book of Psalms is often published as an appendix to the New Testament! But even in that familiarity, the great Old Testament theologian Claus Westermann was absolutely right when he said, "the Psalms belong to a world which is no longer our world."[2] Temples and priests; animal sacrifices, blood, and "drink offerings"; the intimate cohabitation of church and state—these are all so unfamiliar to the twenty-first-century believer that the substance behind these hymns and laments, the imagery deployed in these songs of praise is often beyond our grasp. Think about it. This hymnbook of ancient Israel emerges from a world that ceased to exist more than 2,000 years ago! That's a long time. But the faith, the fear, the celebration, and the sorrow of the ancients—that, somehow, has not ceased to exist. Rather, as Athanasius said, "The Psalms have a unique place in the Bible because [whereas] most of Scripture speaks to us, the Psalms speak for us."[3] The Psalms speak *for* us. And for those of you who are seasoned Christ-followers, you *so* know this. In that dark night of the soul, when my heart is overcome, Psalm 62 reminds me that I hold the hand of the Almighty: "Truly he is my rock and my salvation" and regardless of the locked doors, the lies, corruption, and betrayal all around me, "I will never be shaken" (v. 2). When the tears keep coming, and the loss simply cannot be eased, Psalm 88 cries *with* me: "my eyes are dim with grief. I call to you, Lord, every day!" (v. 9). When the evil around me threatens to destroy everything I've loved and labored for, Psalm 124 reminds me who is on my side. And when the inconceivable has actually come to pass, when the impossible is in my hands, Psalm 126 celebrates with me, "[I was] like those

---

[1] Unfortunately, these quotations from the book of Psalms have been removed. Olsen, "Officials Erode Psalm Displays at Grand Canyon."

[2] Westermann, *The Psalms*, 11.

[3] Athanasius of Alexandria (born c. 296–298 BCE, died 373 CE), was the twentieth bishop of Alexandria, a Christian theologian, a church father, and the chief defender of Trinitarianism against the heresy of Arianism. He served valiantly at the First Council of Nicaea and suffered five exiles at the hands of resistant Roman emperors and corrupt churchmen.

who dreamed. . . . The LORD has done great things for [me]" (vv. 1, 3). Blessed be his name! The Psalms pray *for us*. So, in putting this curriculum into video and paper form, my wish for you and your group is that this deep dive into the book of Psalms will do three things: (1) it will help us reconnect with our ancestors in the faith as they tutor us in what honest faith in hard times looks like; (2) as our ancestors in the faith share their experience of praise and lament with us, we will be reminded of who we are and who God is; and (3) in this discipleship, we will find that we do not walk alone, but we will all find our way back to the Lord of Heaven and Earth who has never ceased to hear the cries of his people.

SESSION 1

The Hymnbook of Ancient Israel

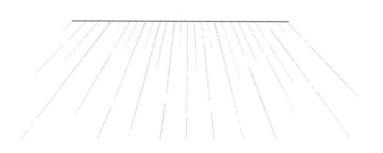

SESSION 1: GROUP MEETING

Schedule

GROUP MEETING

Session 1 Video Teaching and Discussion

INDIVIDUAL STUDY

Day 1: A Prayer

Day 2: The Collection

Day 3: The Content

Day 4: A Psalm

Getting Started

Welcome to the *Epic of Eden: Psalms!* I am so grateful you have chosen this study and I am thrilled to go on this adventure together. We begin with an introductory video teaching, gathering us all onto the same page of both history and biblical text. Following the video, you will engage in what I'm certain will be rich and exciting group discussion sharing what you know already of the psalms and what you are most looking forward to learning.

Along this journey, I encourage you to take part in as much of the personal, individual study as you have time for. As a biblical scholar and professor, my joy comes from doing the heavy lifting of decades of research and study so that I can pass along the wonder of Scripture to you in these pages and provide the framework for you to grow closer to God's Word as a serious believer and follower of Jesus Christ!

After your leader sets up the groundwork for our time together and reviews the weekly schedule, briefly introduce yourselves. Then discuss the **Debrief & Discover** questions below before watching the Session 1 Video Teaching. After the video you will have group discussion in the **Dialogue & Digest** section before closing your gathering with doxology and prayer.

Debrief & Discover

What is the first thing that comes to mind when you think about the book of Psalms?

What is it that makes the psalms special?

Watch Session 1 Video:
THE HYMNBOOK OF ANCIENT ISRAEL
(28 minutes)

Video Notes

These are provided for you and your group members to follow along during the video as well as to offer room for note taking (writing down questions and aha moments as you like).

I.   What is the book of Psalms?

    A.   *tehilim* = "songs" or "praises"

    B.   A culled collection

    C.   A hymnbook: collects and organizes everything a congregation needs in order to worship as a congregation

II. How were the psalms used?

    A.   Examples from our hymnals

        1.   Easter

        2.   Christmas

        3.   Communion

        4.   Marriage

    B.   Examples from the book of Psalms

        1.   Hymns

        2.   Laments

        3.   Liturgical readings

        4.   Enthronement psalms

III.   What was the function of the Psalms?

"In their feasts and fasts, their daily worship, and their special celebrations, the people of Israel remembered and relived God's past victories, committed themselves to present obedience of the covenant laws, which called for full loyalty to Yahweh, and anticipated future triumphs, especially the ultimate defeat of Yahweh's foes."[4]

IV.   How is the collection structured?

V.   What is the point of the structure?

    A. Psalm 1 is a Torah psalm; our foundation, our past

    B. Psalm 2 is a Messianic psalm; our hope, our future

---

[4]   LaSor, Hubbard, and Bush, *Old Testament Survey*, 443.

Dialogue, Digest & Do

Discuss the following as a group.

○ Sandy quotes the fourth-century church father Athanasius saying: "The Psalms have a unique place in the Bible because [whereas] most of Scripture speaks to us, the Psalms speak *for* us." How have you found this to be true in your own life?

○ Describe the most powerful worship experience you've ever had or witnessed. What made it so powerful?

○ Sandy describes the book of Psalms as the hymnbook of ancient Israel. Describe how this hymnbook compares and contrasts to our modern hymnbooks.

○ Review the structure of the book of Psalms. What does Sandy say this structure tells us?

Read Psalm 150, the doxology of doxologies, aloud going around the group reading verse by verse.

Next Week

Next week we'll dig into the book of Psalms and find answers to the questions *who wrote these psalms?* and *why did they write them?*

Closing Prayer

Ask your group members if there is anything they would like prayer for—especially something highlighted by this week's video.

SESSION 1: INDIVIDUAL STUDY

The Hymnbook of Ancient Israel: Who Wrote the Psalms and Why?

Welcome to lesson one! This week in your homework you will be interacting with material from two of the video sessions. (This is the only lesson that relates to two video sessions.) Your first two days of study will cover information discussed in video session one, "The Hymnbook of Ancient Israel," which you have already seen, so it will be mostly review for you. Day three's study will then focus on the upcoming session two video, "Who Wrote the Psalms and Why?" And, finally, day four's study will introduce you to our first "bonus psalm"! The bonus psalm is for those who have enough time for a little extra study and prayer, but there's no shame if you need to skip it.

A Word from Sandy

In the course of putting this curriculum together I wrote to several career worship leaders in my world, asking them why they thought the people of God "need to sing." Why do we write songs, why do we collect those written by our forebearers, and why do we sing them as a congregation? Why was it that the first thing the Israelites did as they stood looking back at the Red Sea—which had just closed over the heads of their oppressors—was *sing*? Why is it that Paul and Silas, beaten and bleeding in the bowels of a Roman prison, were *singing* when the earthquake rattled the doors at midnight? Why are we commanded to *sing* to God and to each other (Eph 5:19; Col 3:16)? And why is it that the *first* thing we do when we gather as the community of faith is *sing*?

Marty Parks, author, composer, and director of a slew of your favorite anthems and cantatas (you can find him at martyparks.com), says this: "Music, like all art, sorta bypasses the intellect and goes straight to the heart."[5] I so agree. Music sneaks past our barriers, captures our attention when we are not offering it, and lays ahold of our souls. It speaks to us in a language we cannot resist. And when the right lyric is set to the right melody, animated by the right instrumentation . . . magic. When all of this is utilized to declare God's Word to his people? Here is strength. And when the people of God come together in this extraordinary space and declare their shared story in song? Here is power. Here is a joy that heals and transforms. This is why we sing. This is why we sing *together*. And this is why we cull our songs until we have a hymnbook that embodies who we were, who we are, and who we pray we will be.

---

[5] Personal communication.

Day 1: A Prayer

Real Time & Space

As LaSor, Hubbard, and Bush note in their well-worn survey of the Old Testament, the Jerusalem temple must have been a busy place. The law prescribed daily services in the morning and at sundown (Exod 29:38–42; Num 28:2–8), sabbath rituals (Num 28:9f.), and special burnt offerings at the new moon (Num 28:11–15; cf. Hos 2:11). The Pilgrim festivals and high holidays were celebrated here, as well as daily special sacrifices for illness, vows fulfilled, personal celebration, and uncleanness. Those who lived nearby may have used the temple precinct for special family occasions. Public events such as the coronation of a king, a victory in battle, or relief from drought or plague would all gather the populace to the temple as well.

Annual feasts could last for several days and drew pilgrims to Jerusalem from throughout Israel: the combined feasts of Unleavened Bread and Passover in early spring (Exod 23:15; Lev 23:5); the feast of Weeks (a harvest festival in late spring, called "Pentecost" in the New Testament; Exod 23:16; 34:22; Num 28:26; Acts 2:1); and the feast of Tabernacles in early fall (also called Booths or Ingathering; Exod 23:16; 34:22; Deut 16:16).[6]

The temple was staffed by the priests and Levites. We will look at the role of the priests in another lesson. For now it is important to know that the Levites, our "second caste" of priests, did everything from putting up and tearing down the Tabernacle tent, to crowd control on holy days (1 Chr 23:2–9), to setting up the sound system and rehearsing the praise band! Among these were two very important family guilds of temple musicians, the "sons of Asaph" and the "sons of Korah."

Asaph is named in 1 Chronicles 6:39; 15:17–19; 16:4–7; and 2 Chronicles 29:30. He was a Levite and a leader in the first choir David recruited to facilitate worship in Jerusalem. The "sons of Asaph" were famous for their musical service in the temple. "These are the men David put in charge of the music in the house of the Lord after the ark came to rest there. They ministered with music before the tabernacle, the tent of meeting, until Solomon built the temple of the Lord in Jerusalem. They performed their duties according to the regulations laid down for them" (1 Chr 6:31–32). Psalms 50, 73–83 are among the psalms of Asaph.

The "sons of Korah" were another family guild, singers from the Kohathite division of Levites (1 Chr 6:33–48; cf. 2 Chr 9:17–19 and 2 Chr 20:19). If this group is descended from the same Korah as Moses's nephew,

---

6   LaSor, Hubbard, and Bush, *Old Testament Survey*, 441–42.

then this is also the family that led a revolt against Moses in the wilderness (Num 16:31–33). But notice how the book of Numbers is careful to point out that Korah's children were spared God's judgment (26:11). Like many Levites, these guys were guards and porters in the tabernacle and were responsible for "things that were baked in the pans"—in other words, grain offerings (1 Chr 9:31; cf. Lev 2:1–10). The psalms attributed to this guild include Psalms 42; 44–49; 84–85; 87–88. The first three are placed in the collection of David.

First Contact

Several years ago, my husband and I were gifted with Ben Patterson's *Praying the Psalms*. What a delightful little book! Each day Ben (retired campus pastor of Hope and Westmont colleges) offers a psalm for reading as well as brief words of wisdom regarding how that psalm speaks into our world today. For a full year Steve and I used this book for our daily devotions. Each day we prayed with Ben, and each day the ancients prayed with us. We learned by experience what Father Patrick Reardon (pastor of All Saints Orthodox Church in Chicago) claims, "Christ walks within the psalms."[7] We were strengthened, challenged, and encouraged. Who was speaking to our hearts during this year-long discipleship? Was it the young psalmist David as he scrambled to survive Saul's murderous jealousy (Ps 63); was it Ben Patterson and his hard-won life wisdom; or was it perhaps, the Word made flesh who held David's hand . . . and holds ours as well?

Into the Book

In the words of the Psalms we hear the cries of the psalmists' hearts. We hear their praise and worship; we hear of their victories and defeats; and we often get a glimpse into their souls.

Read Psalm 32. As you do, notice the divisions throughout the psalm. For example: How does the psalm begin? How does it end? What happens in between?

---

[7]   Reardon, *Christ in the Psalms*, wxvi.

Psalm 32

[1] Blessed is the one
>   whose transgressions are forgiven,
>   whose sins are covered.

[2] Blessed is the one
>   whose sin the LORD does not count against
>   them
>   and in whose spirit is no deceit.

[3] When I kept silent,
>   my bones wasted away
>   through my groaning all day long.

[4] For day and night
>   your hand was heavy on me;
my strength was sapped
>   as in the heat of summer.

[5] Then I acknowledged my sin to you
>   and did not cover up my iniquity.
I said, "I will confess
>   my transgressions to the LORD."
And you forgave
>   the guilt of my sin.

[6] Therefore let all the faithful pray to you
>   while you may be found;
surely the rising of the mighty waters
>   will not reach them.

[7] You are my hiding place;
>   you will protect me from trouble
>   and surround me with songs of
>   deliverance.

[8] I will instruct you and teach you in the way
>   you should go;
>   I will counsel you with my loving
>   eye on you.

[9] Do not be like the horse or the mule,
>   which have no understanding
but must be controlled by bit and bridle
>   or they will not come to you.

[10] Many are the woes of the wicked,
>   but the LORD's unfailing love
>   surrounds the one who trusts in him.

[11] Rejoice in the LORD and be glad, you
>   righteous;
>   sing, all you who are upright in heart!

○ Draw a line between each of the divisions.

○ Give a short title to each division.

○ Notice the progression throughout the psalm. Circle the words that indicate the progression of the psalmist's journey.

○ Choose a color to highlight the words describing the psalmist's condition in verses 3 and 4.

○ Now choose another (happier) color to highlight the words describing his condition as a result of his action taken in verse 5 (don't forget to look at verses 1 and 2!).

○ What does the psalmist encourage his readers to do and not do? Underline those words.

Real People, Real Places, Real Faith

One of the things to keep in mind as we begin our journey into the book of Psalms is that these psalms were written by real people, in real places, struggling with real faith. The superscript of Psalm 32 tells us that our psalm for this lesson is a psalm "of David" (ledawid). The Hebrew is made up of a preposition (le) attached to the name "David," thus the literal translation is "belonging to David." But the exact meaning of the phrase is unclear. Is this "authored by David," "dedicated to David," or "belonging to the Davidic collection"? We don't know. But what we do know is that seventy-three songs are attributed to David in this way. Seventy-three. What this tells us is that David was a man of worship. A man who loved his God and was not at all shy to say so. In the psalms we hear David's petitions, his confessions, and his celebration of God's faithfulness. As a result, we are privileged to pray *with* him, and we are challenged to be *like* him—a people who cry out to God in our brokenness and our joy.

Mosaic image of king David playing the lyre, from a 6th century A.D. synagogue in Gaza.

Our People, Our Places, Our Faith

When I began putting this curriculum on paper, I posted an inquiry to my Facebook page: "What is your favorite psalm, and why?" A friend and colleague from my days at Wheaton College named Psalm 32 as "her" psalm and posted this in response:

> After living a life far from God during most of my 20s, when I became a mother in my 30s I found my way back to the church and Jesus. Life was good now, right? Not quite. In my 40s I finally had to come face-to-face with the sin of those early years. The shame I had carried for so long was just more than I could bear. God was so good to put me in places where I could process through that. Where I could fully experience God's love for me, something I had never been able to imagine.
>
> It began in a women's Bible study when my leader asked us to close our eyes and imagine what it would be like when we first met God in heaven. The tears came quickly. I couldn't even imagine looking upon his goodness. I saw myself turned away, not even able to lay my eyes upon him.
>
> After some really hard work, a lot of time in the Scripture, and some providential sermons, I knew I wanted to confess my sin out loud. That tangible act felt really important. As part of that confession, I read Psalm 32. Those words around God's forgiveness were a balm to my soul.
>
> Dee Pierce 2020
> Director of the Center for Vocation and Career
> Wheaton College

Let me challenge you, right now, to do what Dee did. It is true that when we keep silent about our sin—shove it down, box it up, and bury it—our sin eats away at our souls like a cancer. But it is also true that if we are faithful to confess our sins, he is faithful to forgive. Indeed, as the book of Galatians tells us, "It is for freedom that Christ set us free" (Gal 5:1). So, let's be free.

Read the psalm on pg 12 again, out loud, and with each corresponding line respond:

Verses 1–2:   It is true, how "blessed is the one whose transgressions are forgiven"!

Verses 3–4:   I will no longer be silent.

Verse 5:   Confess your sin and be assured that He forgives.

Verses 6–7:   I don't care what the rest of the world knows or thinks they know. "You are my hiding place."

Verse 8:   Create in me a clean heart, oh God, change me, conform me to the image of the Son (Rom 8:29).

Verse 9:   I will not be a stubborn mule, an untrainable beast.

Verses 10–11:   This is my inheritance, and I will not allow anything or anyone to rob me of it! I will be glad in the Lord, I will shout for joy that I am forgiven and free!

If you are comfortable, share this moment with a friend you trust. Let this be the day when the power of darkness is shattered and the hope of a new day dawns.

Day 2: The Collection

First Contact

Confession time—I can get lost in a paper bag. During my first summer working at the Teen Challenge Women's Home in downtown Philadelphia, the higher-ups finally gave up on sending me out for errands. It wasn't because I was unwilling or irresponsible. I had a car and a great work ethic. They stopped sending me out because . . . well, I would never come back. A seemingly innocuous run to the hardware store could result in three hours of desperate left-hand turns around the city. I am grateful to say that later in my emerging adulthood I discovered this amazing thing called a MAP—that ingenious contribution to the well-being of humanity that puts all the streets and highways on paper! I LOVE maps! Not only because they help me find my way home from the hardware store, but because they offer the big picture. In my opinion, an essential aspect of understanding just about anything. A map lets you see how everything fits together—side streets, highways, city, and open space. Oh, how I love seeing my world coordinated to the page in front of me. And guess what? Once I get a picture of the terrain into my brain . . . I stop getting lost.

Into the Book

Did you know that the book of Psalms is actually made up of five different books? Did you know that each of those five books ends the same way? With a brief but beautiful doxology. Did you also know that many of the psalms contain a superscript that names the author (or compiler), the type of psalm, its liturgical function, the instruments used to accompany the psalm, and/or historical information about the piece? A few psalms even contain a postscript. Today's study will take you on a tour of the book of Psalms. The goal? To coordinate all these signposts to the larger structure of the book so that you won't ever get lost on the way back from the hardware store again.

Open your Bible to Psalm 1. Look just above the title. What is the first thing you notice in the heading? "Book I," right? Working from the video lecture, flip through the book of Psalms and find where each of the five books begins and ends.

Write out the doxology that concludes each book. Complete the following chart as you do. This will be your "map" to the book of Psalms.

BOOK NUMBER	PSALMS	DOXOLOGY
I	1–41	Praise be to the Lord, the God of Israel, from everlasting to everlasting. Amen and Amen. (Ps. 41:13)
II		
III		
IV		
V		

Next, go back through the book of Psalms and read some of the superscripts (the words written above the first line of the psalm, often beginning with "for the director of music" or a psalm of . . ."). As you do, see if you can find and list here:

⭕ Five different authors

⭕ Three different sets of instructions for the director of music

⭕ Five different types of psalms

Real People, Real Places, Real Faith

As you worked your way through the superscripts and postscripts, you no doubt ran into some unfamiliar stuff. For example, in yesterday's study of Psalm 32, the superscript tells the reader what type of psalm it is—a *maskil*. This term is used of thirteen psalms. Its exact meaning is unclear, but some suggestions include "memory verse," "contemplation," or "wisdom song put to music."[8] Another term found all over the psalms is selah (*sela*). This one is used more than seventy times in the Psalter. Most believe it refers to some sort of cessation in the singing or recitation of the psalm that makes space for an instrumental interlude, a response from the choir, or an interjection by the liturgist. Did it surprise you to find that the ancients had a "director of music"? Have you ever thought about the temple having a "worship pastor," choirs, and choir directors? What does that tell you about the setting and function of these songs?

---

8   *HALOT* 1:641; Holladay, 217; LaSor, Hubbard, and Bush, *Old Testament Survey,* 444.

As you likely observed, the superscript "for the director of music" occurs frequently in the superscripts of the psalms. In fact, according to Bruce Waltke, this phrase occurs fifty-five times. After investigating the hymns and laments found in other biblical books,[9] and comparing these with their ancient Near Eastern counterparts, Waltke made an interesting discovery. He found that the phrase "for the director of music" and other information pertaining to the liturgical performance of a psalm (the accompanying instruments or the recommended tune) always appeared in other texts at the *end* of the psalm. In these other musical pieces (in and out of the Bible) the material at the *beginning* of the psalm consisted of information about the genre and the author (such as "a psalm of David"). Thus, Waltke proposed that the superscript "for the director of music" that we read in our Bibles at the beginning of a psalm is actually the postscript of the *previous* psalm,[10] and that these notations were somehow merged in the transference of the book. There are major Bible translation committees that are investigating the feasibility of changing this in your English Bible! For instance, using Psalm 58 as an example, the words "a psalm of David" at the beginning of the psalm should indeed be read as its superscript. But the words, "for the director of music, sung to the tune of 'Do Not Destroy'" should be read as the postscript of Psalm 57. Kind of mind-blowing, yes? What does this mean for you and me? Well, it certainly doesn't alter the contents of the psalms, and I'd encourage us to leave the ultimate placement of these notations to Waltke. But I'd also encourage you to see that your book of Psalms really is a *functioning* hymnal. Just like the songs in your hymnal (or PowerPoint slides!), a worship song should be visibly attributed to its correct author (copyright!), and the hows and whens and wheres of performing the song must be attended to by the worship leader.

---

[9] See for example, Exod 15:1; Judg 5; 2 Sam 18; Job 31:40b; Isa 38:19b; Hab 3:19b.

[10] Waltke, "Superscripts, Postscripts, or Both," 583–96.

Our People, Our Places, Our Faith

In an essay he published in 2005, Walter Brueggemann speaks of the difficulty of preaching the Psalms. In his introduction he speaks of the Psalms being "too"—*too* abrupt and disjunctive, *too* abrasive, *too* emotional, *too* "filled with embarrassing passion," and *too* linked to now defunct cultic practices.[11] As I ponder this observation, I think of the last time I made one of my "emergency" phone calls to my lifelong comrade at arms, Sara King. I think of how I totally let whatever it was rip, venting about whatever absurdity, frustration, or injustice was taking over my world that particular week. I think about how abrupt, disjunctive, abrasive, and "filled with embarrassing passion" those conversations always are. But my friend listens hard, steps into my space with the empathy and accountability that only a long-lived friendship has—and talks me down off the ledge. Do you have one of those friends? If not, you need one!

Then I think of the last time I dropped to my knees, outraged at the latest absurdity, frustration, or injustice taking over my world and ranted to the Almighty. Demanding that he SEE my circumstances and RESPOND! Abrupt, disjunctive, "filled with embarrassing passion." Yes, that is what the Psalms are, because they are real. The real emotions of real people trying to live a real life of faith in the midst of a very real fallen world. And those people are our people. Those prayers are our prayers. Real life is not easily domesticated. And neither are the psalms.

---

[11] Brueggemann, "Psalms in Narrative Performance."

Day 3: The Content

First Contact

At a lecture I was privileged to attend at Harvard Divinity School back in the days of my PhD program, the evangelical church historian, Mark Noll, gave a presentation I will never forget.[12] Noll had been invited to do the impossible: to inaugurate a new Evangelical Chair of Theology at Harvard Divinity without offending anyone. As the historical Christian faith is exclusive, and Harvard Divinity is not, the chances of this going well were pretty slim. But Noll managed to openly affirm historical, evangelical faith and *not* offend the very progressive crowd sitting in front of him. How did he do that? He (brilliantly) let our *hymnody* do the talking. This hymnody—consider Charles Wesley ("Come, O My Guilty Brethren, Come") and Augustus Montague Toplady ("The Old Rugged Cross")—is not only beautiful . . . it has content.

Into the Book

Read Psalm 19 out loud.

Psalm 19

A psalm of David.

1 The heavens declare the glory of God;
　　the skies proclaim the work of his hands.

2 Day after day they pour forth speech;
　　night after night they reveal knowledge.

3 They have no speech, they use no words;
　　no sound is heard from them.

4 Yet their voice goes out into all the earth,
　　their words to the ends of the world.
In the heavens God has pitched a tent for the
　　sun.

---

12 See Mark Noll, "We Are What We Sing," 40.

⁵ It is like a bridegroom coming out of his
      chamber,
    like a champion rejoicing to run his course.

⁶ It rises at one end of the heavens
    and makes its circuit to the other;
    nothing is deprived of its warmth.

⁷ The law of the LORD is perfect,
    refreshing the soul.

The statutes of the LORD are trustworthy,
    making wise the simple.

⁸ The precepts of the LORD are right,
    giving joy to the heart.
The commands of the LORD are radiant,
    giving light to the eyes.

⁹ The fear of the LORD is pure,
    enduring forever.
The decrees of the LORD are firm,
    and all of them are righteous.

¹⁰ They are more precious than gold,
    than much pure gold;
they are sweeter than honey,
    than honey from the honeycomb.

¹¹ By them your servant is warned;
    in keeping them there is great reward.

¹² But who can discern their own errors?
    Forgive my hidden faults.

¹³ Keep your servant also from willful sins;
    may they not rule over me.

Then I will be blameless,
    innocent of great transgression.

¹⁴ May these words of my mouth and this
      meditation of my heart
    be pleasing in your sight,
    LORD, my Rock and my Redeemer.

Now read the psalm again. This time respond to the questions below.

○ For each of verses 1–6, indicate the <u>subject</u>, highlighted verb, and object by <u>underlining</u>, highlighting or circling them.

○ What is happening in verses 1–6?

○ In verses 7–10, using the same method as in the previous verses, indicate the subject, verb, and adjectives.

○ To what are the subjects of verses 7–9 being compared in verse 10?

○ What is their purpose?

○ What is the psalmist's prayer and desire?

○ Who is the focus of this psalm?

Real People, Real Places, Real Faith

The superscripts in the Psalter show us over and over again that the majority of the psalms were meant to be sung. Some of the instructions include the instruments to be used, while others name a particular tune for accompaniment. Julie Tennent of Asbury Theological Seminary, who is herself a very accomplished musician, decided a number of years ago it was time to take these ancient instructions seriously. Her thesis? "The Psalms are for singing—so why don't we sing them?"[13] The result was an Asbury Spring Reader entitled, *Sing*. Here Tennent provides three different tune options for singing each of the psalms. And she challenges us to *do* it. Sing the psalms! Tennent claims that "[i]t is as though the act of singing bridges a distance between us and the text, enabling us to enter into the world of the psalmist."[14] I completely concur, but would like to add that singing these ancient prayers also enables the ancients to enter our world and stand with us in our own joys and challenges.

Go to **http://psalms.seedbed.com/** and navigate your way to Psalm 19. Choose one (or try all three) of the tune options there and sing, yes, *sing* the words of this psalm!

---

[13]   Tennent, Sing: "Singing the Psalms."
[14]   Tennent, Sing: "Singing the Psalms," 4.

Our People, Our Places, Our Faith

On a website titled, "It's All About Me," the author has this to say about the human ego: "While necessary in moderation, allowing one's ego to become overinflated leads to self-centered and downright embarrassing behavior. Such an excess of self-importance can be called egotism."[15] Ah, the oldest crime in the book. The sin foundational to all sin. "It's all about me!" What absurdities have arisen from that foolish posture. And what beauty arises when we resist that posture! Indeed, one of the glories of Christian worship is that for a few bright and shining moments we humans join our voices to declare, "No, no it's not!" So, what a bummer it is when we transform even our worship songs into a recitation of self. There are some songs you could sing to Jesus or your boyfriend and no one could tell the difference. This sort of music is one of my all-time pet peeves.

When an entire worship set is all about how I *feel* today, then we can be assured that the congregation will leave church knowing nothing more than they knew when they walked through the door. Worse, they will leave their encounter with the Creator of the cosmos having ignored him and focused only on their own very limited perspective. A diet of cotton-candy, feel-good lyrics is just as detrimental to the growth of a congregation as a steady diet of Sour Patch Kids and Almond Joys are to your seven-year old. Sure, having a candy bar for lunch makes you feel great for about ten minutes, but (to switch metaphors) it is not going to give you the endurance you need to face the dark night of the soul. Rather, when it's 3 a.m., and I'm in the ICU holding the hand of someone I love, and all I can hear around me are the beeps and whirring of life-support machines, the lyrics of "Jesus or My Boyfriend" songs are useless. No, I need to be reminded of the mighty acts of God. I need to hear that God is near from someone who knows of what they speak. I need lyrics that challenge my anxious perspective and catapult me into *his* perspective. And I need to know that the God I am praying to is the one who parted the Red Sea and raised Lazarus from the dead. When real life happens, cotton-candy lyrics are not going to do it.

I've been on this soap box long enough that one of my students finally decided it was high time I have my very own "Jesus Is My Boyfriend" song. So, with his permission, I thought you might enjoy having your very own copy of Kevin Peake's "Jesus Is My Boyfriend." (Thanks, Kevin!)

---

[15] https://tvtropes.org/pmwiki/pmwiki.php/Main/ItsAllAboutMe

Jesus Is My Boyfriend[16]

I remember the first time you asked me out
To be with you makes me shout.
With all I feel it's too much to say,
You never even make me pay.

CHORUS

Even when we sit down to eat,
I'm reminded of our *berit*.
If I look good or I'm a slob,
It's nice to be in the *bet'ab*

CHORUS

Jesus, thank you for the call
I give you my all and all.
Being with you has no end,
Because Jesus you're my boyfriend!

—bkp

Downright embarrassing, isn't it? And worse, with a catchy tune and the right instrumentation I'm sure we could get it published! So we circle back and ask, what is the real purpose of worship? As Samuel Terrien says: "A service of adoration does not primarily aim at edifying, elevating, purifying or consecrating the worshipers. To be sure, it should bring about all these results, but they are only its by-products. The purpose of worship is to ascribe glory to God." Yes, that is the objective of a worship service. Anything less is not only an affront to God, but it defrauds the people of God.[17] Let's see what we can do to move in that direction.

---

[16]   Used by permission.
[17]   Terrien, *The Psalms and Their Meaning*, xi.

Day 4: a Psalm

First Contact

As noted in the introduction, the day four studies are what we've called bonus psalms. As such I've designed the day four studies a bit differently than the other three days. Each of these studies will still consist of a "First Contact" section. After that the psalm of the day will be presented, followed by a section called "Reading and Observing." In this section, I will lead you through a close read of the psalm by asking in-depth observation questions. Finally, a "Responding" section will offer you multiple ways in which you can respond to the psalm. Over the course of the eight lessons you will dig into psalms from each of the five books of the Psalms, including several different types of psalms (hymns, prayers, thanksgiving, etc.). Remember these are bonus psalms so there is no pressure to complete these prior to viewing the upcoming video.

Read through Psalm 96 once (preferably out loud) without stopping to take notes. Then follow the instructions in Reading & Observing in your second reading.

Psalm 96

¹ Sing to the LORD a new song;
    sing to the LORD, all the earth.

² Sing to the LORD, praise his name;
    proclaim his salvation day after day.

³ Declare his glory among the nations,
    his marvelous deeds among all peoples.

⁴ For great is the LORD and most worthy
    of praise;
    he is to be feared above all gods.

⁵ For all the gods of the nations are idols,
    but the LORD made the heavens.

⁶ Splendor and majesty are before him;
    strength and glory are in his sanctuary.

⁷ Ascribe to the LORD, all you families of
    nations,
    ascribe to the LORD glory and strength.

⁸ Ascribe to the LORD the glory due his name;
    bring an offering and come into his courts.

⁹ Worship the LORD in the splendor of his
    holiness;
    tremble before him, all the earth.

¹⁰ Say among the nations, "The LORD reigns."
    The world is firmly established, it cannot
    be moved;
    he will judge the peoples with equity.

¹¹ Let the heavens rejoice, let the earth be glad;
    let the sea resound, and all that is in it.

¹² Let the fields be jubilant, and everything in
    them;
    let all the trees of the forest sing for joy.

¹³ Let all creation rejoice before the LORD, for
    he comes,
    he comes to judge the earth.
He will judge the world in righteousness
    and the peoples in his faithfulness.

Reading & Observing

Read through the psalm again, this time looking for these things:

○ Which collection does the psalm belong to (Book I, II, III, IV, V)?

○ Is there is a superscript? If so, what is it? Who is the psalm attributed to?

○ What type of psalm is it? (What is the psalmist doing: praying, praising, complaining, giving thanks, etc.?)

Verses 1–3   Notice the verbs in verses 1–3. What does the psalmist instruct his readers/listeners to do? Highlight the verbs the psalmist uses. Underline the object of each verb.

Verses 4–6   Circle the reasons the psalmist provides in these verses for the instructions that he gives in verses 1–3.

Verses 7–10   Highlight the verbs the psalmist uses in verses 7–10. What does the psalmist instruct his readers/listeners to do? Underline the objects of each verb. Who are these instructions addressed to?

Verses 11–13   Who or what are these instructions addressed to? What are they supposed to do? Circle the reason.

Responding

When I read this psalm, I want to respond. I anticipate you feel the same way. Choose one (or more) of the following to participate in the words of the psalmist: pray his prayer, sing his song, and embed these truths on your heart.

○ Sing the psalm! Go to **http://psalms.seedbed.com/** and navigate your way to Psalm 96. Choose one (or all) of the tune options there and sing this psalm to the Lord.

○ Illustrate the psalm! Those of you who are artistically inclined might be interested in an ancient and beautiful tradition known as "illuminated manuscripts." This is when a manuscript is rewritten in calligraphy and supplemented with raised and elaborate letters from the text, borders (marginalia), and miniature illustrations. There are pages set aside at the back of the book (pages 209–217) for you to create your own illuminated psalms as well as a sample to get your creative juices flowing.

○ Pray the psalm! Put in your own names and places, and let the ancients pray with you!

○ Memorize a portion of the psalm!

○ Set the psalm to your own music! Let the words find their way into your heart.

> Tips to Memorizing
> ○ Start small
> ○ Write it down
> ○ Say it out loud
> ○ Repeat

SESSION 2

Who Wrote the Psalms & Why?

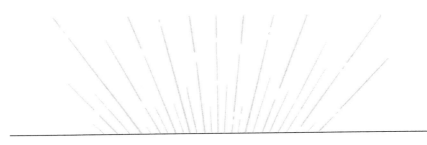

SESSION 2: GROUP MEETING

Schedule

GROUP MEETING
Session 2 Video Teaching and Discussion

INDIVIDUAL STUDY
Day 1: The Presence
Day 2: The Feasts
Day 3: The Songs
Day 4: A Psalm

Debrief & Discover

What is your favorite worship song?

What about it makes it your favorite?

Watch Session 2 Video:
WHO WROTE THE PSALMS & WHY?
(20 minutes)

Video Notes

These are provided for you and your group members to follow along during the video as well as to offer room for note taking (writing down questions and aha moments as you like).

I. David

    A. The New Testament refers to the Psalms as the words of David (Mark 12; Matt 22; Luke 20; Acts 1, 4, 13)

    B. Seventy-three psalms are attributed to David

    C. David is a man of worship

        1. I Samuel 16

        2. I Samuel 18:10

        3. 2 Samuel 1:17–27

4. 2 Samuel 23:1–7

D. David centralized the cult of Israel (*mishkan*, "dwelling place of the Most High")

II. Others

  A. Collectors

  1. David (Pss 3–72)

  2. Korah (Pss 42; 44–49; 84, 85, 87, 88)

  3. Asaph (Pss 50; 73–83)

  B. Authors

  1. Solomon

  2. Ethan the Ezrahite (1 Kgs 4:31)

  3. Heman the Ezrahite

  4. Anonymous

III. What do the Psalms teach us about our worship?

  A. Rehearse the mighty acts of God

  B. Ascribe glory to God

Dialogue, Digest & Do

○ According to Sandy, why should we not be surprised that David is associated with the book of Psalms? What can we learn from David?

○ What do the Psalms have to teach us about our worship?

○ Why is this important?

○ Read and discuss the following quote by Samuel Terrien: "A service of adoration does not primarily aim at edifying, elevating, purifying or consecrating the worshipers. To be sure, it should bring about all these results, but they are only its by-products. The purpose of worship is to ascribe glory to God."

○ What do you think about Sandy's pet peeve: "Jesus Is My Boyfriend" type of songs?

As we saw in the video and in the study guide, "the purpose of worship is to ascribe glory to God." Does this statement challenge you in your own worship? What changes, if any, do you need to make in your own worship?

In your study guide this past week, you were asked to sing Psalm 19 using one of the tune options found at http://psalms.seedbed.com. If your group is willing, sing the psalm together. For the brave at heart, take a video. For those willing to slay a giant, post the video on social media!

Next Week

As we read through the book of Psalms, we'll certainly come across things that make us go "hmm." Next week we'll begin looking into how we interpret the psalms, starting with understanding sacred space.

Closing Prayer

Ask your group members if there is anything they would like prayer for—especially something highlighted by this week's video.

Reminder: If you are behind in the reading, pick up with the individual study tomorrow to get back on track.

SESSION 2: INDIVIDUAL STUDY

Interpreting the Psalms: Sacred Space

A Word from Sandy

I spend a lot of time in Israel. Field archaeology, historical geography, and students of every age mean that I've seen the standard tourist attractions dozens and dozens of times. My favorite? En Gedi. My least favorite? The Church of the Holy Sepulchre. "How can you say that?" you ask. "That ancient church marks the place of Jesus's death and resurrection!" I get it. But it also marks some of the oldest and ugliest conflicts within the supposed Body of Christ. You can find clergy from the Greek Orthodox, Roman Catholic, and Armenian Apostolic churches, as well as the Coptic Orthodox, Syriac Orthodox, and Ethiopian Orthodox. And they are all at each other's throats. So I hate going there.

That was until one summer morning back in 2008 when I went with my daughter. She was almost five. She was also the definition of "the tornado toddler." And the fact that she was suffering through a dig schedule surrounded by graduate students meant that she was sick and tired of "the Holy Land." So much so that the previous evening when we stepped through security onto the plaza of the Western Wall at sundown (that would be Shabbat), after very clear instructions not to leave my side ("if I lose you here, honey, I will never find you again"), she immediately bolted into the crowd of 10,000 strong. Yes, my daughter has the unique privilege of having wailed at the Wailing Wall!

So, I wasn't expecting much the next morning as we were scheduled to visit my least favorite place in all of Israel-Palestine. But oh, how wrong I was. As soon as that tornado toddler walked through the ancient wooden door of the Church of the Holy Sepulchre, something happened. I think it just might have been the presence of the sacred. Eyes transfixed, she made a beeline for the large pink granite slab known as the Stone of Anointing where Jesus's body was supposedly laid out for burial. She approached with awe, kneeled among the pilgrims, and spread herself out over the stone—rubbing the scented olive oil all over her hands and face. Then we sprinted off to the rotunda, where she gazed with wonder at the cathedral ceilings and touched *everything*. I chased her to Calvary where the Greek Orthodox priests, recognizing a Greek child, brought her to the front of the line. She knelt and prayed at the rock of crucifixion. Outside the Roman Catholic

(Franciscan) Chapel of the Nailing of the Cross, she insisted on lighting candles. We must have visited every nook and cranny of that ancient edifice and each time I was stunned by her reaction. What had happened to my distracted, impatient child? As she exclaimed as we exited the church, "Mama, that was the holiest place I've ever been." Sacred space.

Real Time & Space

I find the nature of sacred space in the ancient world fascinating. In his classic work *Ancient Israel: Its Life and Institutions*, the exceptional scholar of Old Testament Roland de Vaux discusses the topic at length. (De Vaux was also a French Dominican priest, director of Ecole Biblique in Jerusalem, and the first director of the Dead Sea Scrolls project.) Here we learn that sacred space in Israel's world was never chosen simply for convenience or preference. Sacred space was the choice of the gods, and in Israel's case the choice of the one, true God. The place was typically indicated by some sort of manifestation of the god's presence—his activity, his appearance, or his directive. So as we rehearse the locations of Israel's central cult site, we find that Israel is directed first to Mount Ebal (Deut 11:29; 27:4), then Shiloh (Josh 18:1), and then to Jerusalem (1 Chr 15:3). As we will rehearse in the video teaching, Deuteronomy 12:1–5 makes it expressly clear that when Israel enters Canaan they are to dismantle the cult sites of the Canaanites, and replace those multiple sites with the one and only site of Yahweh. Why *one* site? To help our heroes hang onto the idea that there is only *one* God.

(above left) A Canaanite Bull figurine. The Canaanite high god El, was represented by a bull, his son Baal by a bull calf. (right) A Stele of Baal, the Canaanite god of fertility and storm depicted with a mace raised in his right hand and a sheaf of wheat in his left.

What did the ancients believe about these sacred sites? They believed that they could meet God there. That this place was the *omphalos* of the universe—a fancy word for "belly button." Like a "belly button" the sacred precinct was that spot where heaven met earth, where the umbilical cord of the cosmos ushered divine power into human space. For the Israelites, this meant that the

Jerusalem temple was the one place where a worshiper could be assured of encountering the Almighty. Why was this site (like Eden and the New Jerusalem to come) holy? Because God was there. And as we look back at Eden and forward to the New Jerusalem, we find that this space is marked by sacred rivers (which bring fertility to the earth), sacred trees, mountains (Mount Sinai and Mount Zion for example), pomegranates, and standing stones (*masseboth*)—all of which helped to mark the space as one where *worship* should

Standing stones (masseboth) from the "high place" in the city of Gezer.

occur. And if Israel destroys the cult sites of the surrounding nations, Israel will not be confused in her singular allegiance to Yahweh or tempted to offer her worship to other gods.

Keep in mind that Israel's sacred space did not necessarily *look* different from that of their neighbors. But who it housed was *very* different. Rather than being occupied by a statue covered in gold and silver, the Holy of Holies was occupied by the all-powerful but invisible God. Rather than a god who was hungry and needed sacrifice to satisfy his cravings, the Jerusalem temple was occupied by a God who "owned the cattle on a thousand hills" and valued obedience far more than sacrifice (Ps 50:10; 1 Sam 15:22). As a result, the means by which Yahweh was worshiped and the expectations he placed on his people were dramatically different than worship practices in Canaan as well.

Day 1: The Presence

First Contact

As I write this, our world is in the midst of a pandemic. Life as we know it has been turned upside down and hundreds of thousands of people have already lost their lives. Families are separated from their loved ones. Babies are being born in silence. Weddings are celebrated without fanfare. Aging parents are isolated in nursing homes, and the closest their people can get is gazing through a door or a window. Perhaps most agonizing, the sick are dying alone. Oh, how we want to be with those we love, but Covid-19 makes access impossible.

Into the Book

If you've read *The Epic of Eden* or have done the *Epic of Eden: Understanding the Old Testament* video study, you'll remember that God's original plan for humanity was that the people of God would live in the place of God dwelling in the presence of God. You'll also recall that as a result of the rebellion in Eden, God drove humanity out of the garden so that they no longer had access to the place of God or the presence of God. As the great Story moves forward, the people of God become the nation of Israel, whom God rescues from slavery in Egypt. And at Mount Sinai Yahweh makes a covenant with his people that begins to restore what has been broken. It is in the book of Exodus where we read Yahweh's rescue plan. And it is to Exodus that we now turn.

Read Exodus 25:8 in at least three different Bible versions.

○ What does God ask Moses to have the people do?

○ Why does God want them to do this?

Now read Exodus 29:45–46.

> [45] Then I will dwell among the Israelites and be their God. [46] They will know that I am the Lord their God, who brought them out of Egypt so that I might dwell among them. I am the Lord their God.

○ Underline the two phrases that are repeated twice in these two verses. What is significant about these words?

Let's turn now to the New Testament and read Luke 8:42b–48 (cf. Matt 9:20–22 and Mark 5:24b–34).

> As Jesus was on his way, the crowds almost crushed him. [43] And a woman was there who had been subject to bleeding for twelve years, but no one could heal her. [44] She came up behind him and touched the edge of his cloak, and immediately her bleeding stopped.
>
> [45] "Who touched me?" Jesus asked.
>
> When they all denied it, Peter said, "Master, the people are crowding and pressing against you."
>
> [46] But Jesus said, "Someone touched me; I know that power has gone out from me."
>
> [47] Then the woman, seeing that she could not go unnoticed, came trembling and fell at his feet. In the presence of all the people, she told why she had touched him and how she had been instantly healed. [48] Then he said to her, "Daughter, your faith has healed you. Go in peace."

○ What is the setting?

○ If you were a Jew in the first century, by what title would you have addressed Jesus?

Read Leviticus 15:25.

○ What is this woman's condition?

○ Do you understand why this woman was disallowed from approaching Jesus openly? What would have been the impact of this woman touching Jesus according to Levitical law?

○ What was the woman seeking from Jesus?

○ What did she do?

○ What was her response when Jesus knew what had happened?

○ What was Jesus's response?

Real People, Real Places, Real Faith

In the Exodus passages above we see for the first time since the garden of Eden that God is dwelling with his people. Yahweh continues to reiterate that he will dwell among them and be their God. In those words, we can hear Yahweh's longing to be with his people. If you continue reading in Exodus 25–31 you will read *how* he intends to be with his people—all the details of the construction of the tabernacle with all its accoutrements. You will also learn that between the Most Holy Place and the Holy Place was a curtain (embroidered with cherubim) behind which the Presence dwelt. You will also learn that the priests were the only ones allowed in the Holy Place, and the high priest alone, once a year, was allowed to enter the Most Holy Place. Another curtain separated the Holy Place from the courtyard—the only place the common worshiper could enter. What does this tell us? Why the curtains and the separation? As I detail in an essay titled, "What Do I Know of Holy? On the Person and Work of the Holy Spirit in Scripture," the irony of the tabernacle is the agony of redemptive history.

For in the tabernacle the Presence was housed in the holy of holies, and thereby was partitioned off from those who would seek to draw near. The increasing sanctification (and therefore restriction) of the outer court, holy place, and holy of holies clearly communicated that only the spiritual elite could enter there. Thus, whereas any clean, worshiping Israelite could enter the outer court, only priests could enter the holy place, and only the High Priest could enter the holy of holies— and that only once per year on the Day of Atonement. This was a day of profound anxiety for the one selected as High Priest, and he went through days of ritual cleansing prior to entering God's Presence. When he entered, he wore bells in order to assure all who listened outside the veil that "he had not died in the Holy Place and that he continued to minister on their behalf" (cf. Exod. 28:31–35). The increasing sanctification of the three areas of the tabernacle, the necessity of mediation and sacrifice, the restricted access and elaborate measures taken for cleansing and atonement all communicate the same message: The Holy One is here. And anyone who draws near must either be holy . . . or dead. By its very existence the tabernacle communicated God's desire for *cohabitation*. While its increasing restriction of persons commensurably communicated the legacy of sin, *separation*. In the Old Covenant, the typical worshiper *never* approached the Presence.[18]

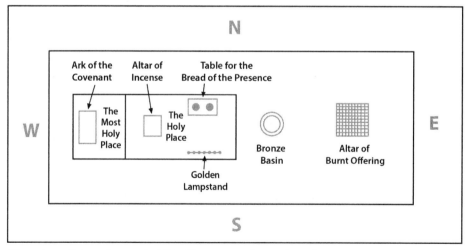

Floorplan of the tabernacle. This illustration shows the relative positions of the tabernacle furniture. See the DVD video for a detailed reconstruction.

---

18   Richter, "What Do I Know of Holy?," 28–29.

Our People, Our Places, Our Faith

How many of us still feel the distance of the tabernacle? Those moments when we simply want to feel the Presence in our space, but instead the sky over our heads feels like bronze (Deut 28:23). When we are convinced that either our sin or God's silence is an impenetrable barrier? Let me remind you of the grand introduction to John's Gospel. Here the Gospel writer is trying to explain to his audience that the incarnation has done it, it is the solution, that the separation of the fall, the estrangement of our rebellion has at last been resolved.

And the best language he can come up with to describe this to his audience is, you guessed it, the language of the tabernacle:

> **The Word became flesh and made his dwelling [literally, "tabernacled"] among us. We have seen his glory, the glory of the one and only Son, who came from the Father, full of grace and truth. (John 1:14)**

Do you hear the language here? No more barriers, no more veil blocking our view, no more separation. We could not go to him, so he came to us. Think of the woman "subject to bleeding for twelve years," introduced to us in Mark 5:25–34 who could not join her family at any holy days in the tabernacle, or around the family table.

What did this mean for her?

What does it mean for you?

Day 2: The Feasts

First Contact

New Year's Day, Valentine's Day, Easter, Memorial Day, the 4th of July, Labor Day, Thanksgiving, and Christmas. These are the days that we in the United States feast. Some of these are sacred days, some are national days. But each marks our calendar with the opportunity to change "everyday" into "something special." How do we make these days special? We anticipate! We decorate! We gather and we eat . . . a lot! There are all sorts of special foods and decorations and activities that come out only on these days that shape our time and space. And for each celebration, there are special memories as well. Indeed, it is memory that shapes the day—not only the memory of *why* we are celebrating (the incarnation, the resurrection, national independence, our veterans), but the memory of past celebrations of the same day. Memory gives these holidays meaning. Family and food make it fun.

Into the Book

In yesterday's study we looked at the tabernacle, the tent in which the presence of God dwelt among his people prior to the building of the temple. It was Solomon who built the temple on Mount Zion in Jerusalem. Three times a year, the Israelites would make their way to Jerusalem to celebrate the three pilgrim feasts. Let's take a look at what those were, what they involved, and what the purpose was.

Complete the table on the following page.

REFERENCES	NAME OF THE FEAST	DESCRIPTION/ SACRIFICES/ OFFERINGS	PURPOSE
Exod 12:1–14; Lev 23:5; Num 9:1–14; 28:16; Deut 16:1–3a, 4b–7	Passover		
Exod 23:16a; 34:22a; Lev 23:15–21; Num 28:26–31; Deut 16:9–12	Weeks (Pentecost) (Harvest)		
Exod 23:16b; 34:22b; Lev 23:33–36a, 39–43 Num 29:12–34; Deut 16:13–15	Tabernacles (Booths) (Ingathering)		

Adapted from LaSor, Hubbard, and Bush, *Old Testament Survey,* 92–93, *NIV Study Bible* (Grand Rapids: Zondervan Bible Publishers).

Real People, Real Places, Real Faith

The temple was Yahweh's "house." Three times a year all of Israel was required to gather at the temple to celebrate who he was and who they were. And yes, *celebration* was the objective. In addition to a celebration of the sacred, most of these holidays were supposed to be fun. The Israelites were commanded to remember and celebrate the exodus from Egypt. They were to joyfully give thanks for the harvest. They were to remember and commemorate the journey from Egypt to the promised land. And as you just discovered, each of these feasts included ritual acts of worship, sacrifice, and offerings. Why sacrifices? Sacrifice was a standard act of worship in the ancient Near East. But whereas Israel's neighbors sacrificed to keep the gods fat and happy (and thereby manipulate the gods into keeping the worshipers fat and happy), Israel sacrificed as an expression of gratitude and deference to Yahweh. For Israel, sacrifice also communicated atonement. Sacrifice was a powerful visual aid that made it expressly clear that in order to approach Yahweh, blood was required. Thus, the citizen of Israel brought a clean animal to Yahweh's house and presented it before the priest. The priest checked the animal to ensure that the citizen had indeed brought his best, and then assisted the citizen in slaughtering the animal. The animal's blood was gathered and ritually dispensed. The meat was butchered: a portion went to God, a portion to the priests who staffed the temple complex, but the bulk was returned to the worshiper. Why? To facilitate the feast! And as the standard slaughtered ewe weighed in at about 100 pounds (35–40 pounds of meat), and a newly weaned male lamb (the most common and coveted sacrifice) at 45 pounds (about 25 pounds of meat), these celebrations could feed as many as 100 adults! "There, in the presence of the Lord your God, you and your families shall eat and shall rejoice in everything you have put your hand to, because the Lord your God has blessed you" (Deut 12:7). The abundance of meat resulting from a sacrifice is one of the reasons why the worshiper is encouraged to include their entire extended household, the widow, the orphan, and the Levite at their table (Deut 12:18–19; 14:27; 26:11–13). *Everyone* is to be included and *everyone* is to experience the blessing of God's provision.

Our People, Our Places, Our Faith

I am often asked if the sacrifice and atonement of the Old Testament actually "worked." In other words, did these ancient sacrifices actually achieve atonement? Well, the New Testament makes it expressly clear that the nexus of all atonement comes from the sacrifice of Christ. As the following passages state:

The death he died, he died to sin once for all. (Rom 6:10)

For Christ also suffered once for sins, the righteous for the unrighteous, that he might bring us to God, being put to death in the flesh but made alive in the Spirit. (1 Pet 3:18)

And by that will, we have been made holy through the sacrifice of the body of Jesus Christ once for all. (Heb 10:10)

Indeed, the source of divine power behind the atonement enacted in the temple was the sacrifice of the God-man Jesus Christ. But as William Dumbrell, the great Reformed theologian, states: "The clear understanding of Leviticus is that sacrifice did effect atonement (Lev 1:4; 4:35), and by sacrifice the worshiper was cleansed and purified from sin. When the worshiper drew near to the sanctuary, killed his own beast, and laid his hand as indication of its substitution for him, he underscored the personal recognition that a breach in relationships had occurred. . . . To suggest that the forgiveness offered through the system was only symbolic or typical reduces sacrifice in the OT to a vague and meaningless ritual. This was never intended."[19] Yes this ancient system "worked," but it worked in anticipation and remembrance (1 Pet 1:18–20) of the breathtaking truth of the gospel, that in Christ, God has died for man.

---

[19]   Dumbrell, *The Faith of Israel*. 42–43.

Day 3: The Songs

First Contact

According to the experts, long-term memory is stored and retrieved by association. That's why if you sprint upstairs to get something, and then realize you can't remember why you sprinted in the first place, if you head BACK downstairs to where you first thought of it, you'll remember what you're looking for. Really frustrating, I know, but of course good for cardio! This is because that *place* holds *memory*. We associate our memories with our places, and revisiting those places triggers the retrieval of memory. Kind of cool, huh?

Into the Book

In day two of individual study one I asked you to look at the superscripts of Psalms. If you made it through all the psalms, you may have noticed that Psalms 120–134 have a similar superscript: "A song of ascents." These were the songs the pilgrims would sing on their way (their "ascent") to Jerusalem three times a year to participate in the great pilgrim feasts. What was the content of these songs? A little more profound than Hannah Montana's "It's All Right Here" (see video teaching), but still the same impact. Let's take a look at a few.

Read through the passages in the chart on the next page and make some observations:

○ What is the psalmist doing (for example, praying, rejoicing, anticipating, etc.)?

○ What does the psalmist declare about Yahweh's character? If he is rejoicing, what is he rejoicing in? If he is anticipating, what is he anticipating?

○ What is the psalmist's posture toward Yahweh?

REFERENCE	PASSAGE	OBSERVATIONS

Ps 120:1–2	¹ I call on the LORD in my distress,
	    and he answers me.
	² Save me, LORD, from lying lips
	    and from deceitful tongues.	

Ps 122:1–4	¹ I rejoiced with those who said to me,
	    "Let us go to the house of the LORD."
	² Our feet are standing
	    in your gates, Jerusalem.
	³ Jerusalem is built like a city
	    that is closely compacted together.
	⁴ That is where the tribes go up—
	    the tribes of the LORD—
	to praise the name of the LORD
	    according to the statute given to Israel.	

Ps 123	¹ I lift up my eyes to you,
	    to you who sit enthroned in heaven.
	² As the eyes of the slaves look to the
	        Hand of their master,
	    As the eyes of a female slave
	        Look to the hand of her mistress
	So our eyes look to the LORD our God,
	    till he shows us his mercy.
	³ Have mercy on us, LORD, have mercy on us,
	    for we have endured no end of contempt.
	⁴ We have endured on end of ridicule from
	        the arrogant,
	    of contempt from the proud.	

REFERENCE	PASSAGE	OBSERVATIONS
Ps 130	[1] Out of the depths I cry to you, LORD; [2] LORD, hear my voice. Let your ears be attentive to my cry for mercy. [3] If you, LORD, kept a record of sins, LORD, who could stand? [4] But with you there is forgiveness, so that we can, with reverence, serve you. [5] I wait for the LORD, my whole being waits, and in his word I put my hope. [6] I wait for the LORD more than watchmen wait for the morning, more than watchmen wait for the morning. [7] Israel, put your hope in the LORD, for with the LORD is unfailing love and with him is full redemption. [8] He himself will redeem Israel from all their sins.	
Ps. 134	[1] Praise the LORD, all you servants of the LORD who minister by night in the house of the LORD. [2] Lift up your hands in the sanctuary and praise the LORD. [3] May the LORD bless you from Zion, he who is the Maker of heaven and earth.	

Real People, Real Places, Real Faith

Christopher Wright speaks of the "holy rhythm" of Israel's life.[20] Every seven days, Sabbath. Every spring, the Feast of Passover/Unleavened Bread (March/April). Every summer, the Feast of Weeks (May/June). Every fall, the Feast of Tabernacles (September). Then came the annual and triennial tithes, and at last the sabbatical years and Year of Jubilee—a "holy rhythm." Similar to the effects of the law on civic life, this holy calendar structured their *time*. Each season was marked by remembrance and expectation: the rehearsal of what God *had* done, thanksgiving for what God *was* doing, and expectation of what God *would* do.

As described in Deuteronomy 16:1–12, the Passover was observed for seven days. The first night always includes a special meal, the *seder*, complete with a liturgy that rehearses the story of the Exodus and engages every member of the family. The objective? That each person around the table personalizes the history—that each feels the agonies of slavery, the joy of release, and the challenges of the journey. Each item of food on the table retells the story (lamb, bitter herbs, *matzah* bread). Each glass of wine marks a juncture in the liturgy. The Feast of Weeks (*Shavuot*) occurs fifty days after Passover. For this reason the New Testament writers spoke of it as Pentecost. This festival celebrates the gift of the Law at Sinai and required two loaves of bread as an offering at the holy place. Current-day Jews also typically pull an all-nighter reading and memorizing Torah. The Feast of Tabernacles commemorates the forty years of wandering and requires every Jewish family to build a "booth" in their yard to remember the tents in the wilderness. Rabbi Jamie Cowen reports that the *sukkah* ("booth") must have at least three sides and a roof to be kosher (usually comprised of tree branches or palm leaves). Modern-day Jews decorate with lights and other festive gear, and tradition requires that all meals be eaten in the booth *all* week. *And* the family must spend at least one night under the stars. What fun! In sum, Israel was required to live a life that never wandered too far from the sacred acts of remembrance, pilgrimage, and celebration that rehearsed to them their great story. And they did all these things within the embrace of community. Can you imagine a *better* plan for keeping a community focused on where they came from and who they are?

So what do you hear in the voices of the pilgrims as they make their journey to the holy place for these celebrations? I hear joy. I hear praise. I hear reverence for the Creator of the cosmos. I hear confidence in Yahweh's faithfulness. I hear gratitude for Yahweh's past actions. And I hear anticipation and expectation for what Yahweh will do in this most recent encounter with him in their shared sacred space.

[20] Wright, *Deuteronomy*, 5.

Our People, Our Places, Our Faith

Psalm 130:5 speaks of a worshiper waiting with "my whole being," and placing their whole hope in "his word." "More than watchmen wait for the morning," (v. 6) says the psalmist, I wait for my God. I don't know about you, but I am by nature a very impatient person. My life motto? *Get it done. Get it done now!* My first response to every crisis is what can I *do?* But the only thing this worshiper is doing is going to where God is and asking him to intervene. And after asking, this worshiper is watching. Watching with eager anticipation like a watchman waiting for the dawn.

So many things can be learned here. First, this worshiper has *gone to where God is* and has boldly asked for aid. I so need to learn this lesson. I'm also struck by the comparison of waiting for the sunrise. If you have ever had a night filled with heartache, anxiety, or sickness, you know all too well what it means to wait for the dawn. Sitting in the dark hours, it is easy for those things that worry or afflict you to seem way bigger and more threatening than they are. And so we tell ourselves, it will be better in the morning. And we are right. But like this worshiper, we have no control over the dawn. All we can do is wait. *But* note that this worshiper is fully convinced that God will answer just as the sunrise *will* come. What a profound expression of confidence. So what do we learn here? When faced with a crisis we go to where God is—be that your prayer closet or the assembly of the saints. Then we ask, boldly. Then we wait . . . and we choose to believe the sun will rise. Why? Because it always has. In other words, we rehearse God's mighty acts in the past, and we believe for his mighty acts in our future—we allow our memory to shape our expectations.

Day 4: A Psalm

First Contact

A dear friend and writing partner, Kathy names one of her favorite things to do in Israel is to hike the Wadi Qelt from Jerusalem to Jericho. A "wadi" is a valley, a ravine really, that is dry except during the rainy season. So think very steep slopes, narrow pathways, loose rocks, and potentially rapidly moving water at the bottom. Now think hot (really hot), dry, and dusty. There is no shade anywhere, so make sure you have your water bottle with you. And good shoes. This hike is going to take you all day. In light of the rigor, why is this one of Kathy's favorite things to do in Israel? One reason is because it is breathtakingly beautiful (especially St. George's Monastery, which is tucked precariously into the steep slope of the wadi). But the main reason is because "as I struggle with the steep and narrow paths, bad footing and loose rocks, high heat, and dirt filling my shoes and wind blowing in my face, I am reminded of what the pilgrims headed to Jerusalem must have experienced. And I'm pretty jazzed to be walking in their steps."

Read through Psalm 121 once (preferably out loud) without stopping to take notes. Then follow the instructions in Reading & Observing in your second reading.

Psalm 121
A song of ascents

¹ I lift up my eyes to the mountains—
    where does my help come from?
² My help comes from the LORD,
    the Maker of heaven and earth.

³ He will not let your foot slip—
    he who watches over you will not slumber;
⁴ indeed, he who watches over Israel
    will neither slumber nor sleep.

⁵ The LORD watches over you—
    the LORD is your shade at your right hand;
⁶ the sun will not harm you by day,
    nor the moon by night.

⁷ The LORD will keep you from all harm—
    he will watch over your life;
⁸ the LORD will watch over your coming
    and going
    both now and forevermore.

Reading & Observing

Read through the psalm again, this time looking for these things:

○ Which collection does the psalm belong to (Book I, II, III, IV, V)?

○ Is there a superscript? If so, what is it? Who is the psalm attributed to?

○ What type of psalm is it? (What is the psalmist doing: praying, praising, complaining, giving thanks, etc.?)

○ What is the significance of the mountains?

○ Who does the psalmist look to for help?

○ Now that you know this is a song of ascent, one of the psalms the pilgrims sang on the often treacherous trek up to Jerusalem, what pilgrimage imagery do you notice in the psalm? <u>Underline</u> that.

○ Highlight the things the psalmist is confident about.

Responding

As Kathy relates: "The words of this psalm have brought peace to my soul on more than one occasion where I literally 'lift[ed] up my eyes to the mountains' for help . . . and 'the Maker of heaven and earth' kept me 'from all harm.' This one is one I've committed to memory."

How do you respond? Choose one (or more) of the following as a response to your study of this psalm.

○ Sing the psalm! Go to **http://psalms.seedbed.com/** and navigate your way to Psalm 121. Choose one (or all) of the tune options there and sing this psalm to the Lord.

○ Illustrate the psalm! Those of you who are artistically inclined might be interested in an ancient and beautiful tradition known as "illuminated manuscripts." There are pages set aside at the back of the book (pages 209–217) for you to create your own illuminated psalms as well as a sample to get your creative juices flowing.

○ Pray the psalm! Put in your own names and places, and let the ancients pray with you!

○ Choose one paragraph of this psalm to memorize.

○ Set this psalm to your own music. Let the words find their way into your heart.

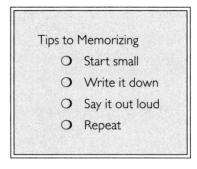

Tips to Memorizing
○ Start small
○ Write it down
○ Say it out loud
○ Repeat

SESSION 3

Interpreting the Psalms: Sacred Space

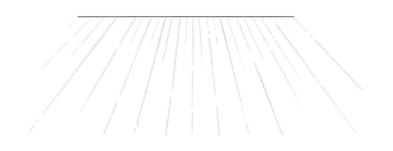

SESSION 3: GROUP MEETING

Schedule

GROUP MEETING
Session 3 Video Teaching and Discussion

INDIVIDUAL STUDY
Day 1: The Officers
Day 2: The Enthronement
Day 3: The Protection
Day 4: A Psalm

Debrief & Discover

Ask your group members to define "sacred space."

What makes space "sacred"?

Watch Session 3 Video:
INTERPRETING THE PSALMS: SACRED SPACE
(26 minutes)

Video Notes

These are provided for you and your group members to follow along during the video as well as to offer room for note taking (writing down questions and aha moments as you like).

Hermeneutics: the science of interpreting Scripture

I. Interpreting the Psalms

   A. The Psalms are historically influenced

   B. The emphasis of the Psalms is experience rather than didactics

   C. The Psalms are poetry

II. The cult of Israel

    A. The central cult site: the tabernacle

        1. Exodus 25:8

        2. Footprint of the tabernacle

            a. Outer court

            b. Holy place

            c. Holy of Holies

        3. Cohabitation and separation

        4. One God, one cult site—Deuteronomy 6:4

    B. The function of the central cult site

        1. The house of the King of Israel

        2. The place of sacrifice and mediation

        3. The place of celebration

III. The function of "place" in memory and expectation

    A. Jeff Malpas: place holds memory

    B. My family's sacred space

IV. The Songs of Ascent (Pss 120–134)

Dialogue, Digest & Do

○ Sandy talks about the function of the central cult site in Israel. What does she say the function was?

○ Sandy says that from an anthropological perspective, the central cult site was the primary unifying factor in Israelite society. How so?

○ How does understanding the idea of sacred space affect your understanding of the psalms?

○ Does your family have "sacred space" somewhere in their lives? How does this effect your experience of time together? If you don't have "sacred space" in what ways do you think the absence of such impacts your family dynamic, worship, or experience of shared faith?

○ In your study guides this past week you looked at a few songs of ascent. What kinds of observations did you make about these psalms?

As you read through the psalms this week remember that Israel's cult site held their memory. We are blessed that we hold in our hands the written memory of their place. May God meet each one of us this week with their memory and may their memory shape our expectations.

Next Week

Have you ever read through the psalms and wondered why there is so much talk of the king and battles? We'll find out why that is next week as we continue our discussion about interpreting the psalms.

Closing Prayer

Ask your group members if there is anything they would like prayer for—especially something highlighted by this week's video. We recommend that your "prayer secretary" keep a running list so that the group can revisit past prayer requests and check in on how things are going. It is a great way for the group to get to know each other and bear each other's burdens.

Reminder: If you are behind in the reading, pick up with the individual study tomorrow to get back on track.

SESSION 3: INDIVIDUAL STUDY

Interpreting the Psalms: Theocracy

A Word from Sandy

In this individual study, we are still talking about "hermeneutics." This seventy-five-cent word simply means "the science of interpreting Scripture." And, yes, contrary to what many people want to believe, there is a science to interpreting Scripture. There are rules to the proper interpretation of any literary piece, and when it comes to biblical exegesis (another seventy-five-cent word), the key to interpretation is *context*: literary context, canonical context, socio-historical context. If a reader is able to place a passage in all of these contexts, they are able to interpret responsibly and insightfully. If not, well, to quote a well-worn proverb whose source I have lost over the years: "A text without a context is just a pretext for whatever it was you wanted to say."

What does this look like on the ground? Well, how many times have you sat through a sermon where you felt the preacher was *using* the Scripture as a launching pad into his/her own topic, as opposed to focusing in on what the biblical author was actually trying to say? In our study, we will be championing the latter (not the former). Thus, as you approach the psalms you need to keep in mind that these pieces are *historically influenced*. We've talked about the influence of Israel's religious system—the tabernacle/temple complex; the mediation accomplished via sacrifice and priesthood; the Pilgrim Feasts; the Songs of Ascent, and the joy, memory, and expectation surrounding a visit to the sacred site. Now we need to talk about the historical influence of Israel's system of government, *theocracy*.

Real Time & Space

What is a theocracy? The word is actually two words: *theos* + *kratos* (<*kratew*) meaning *god* + *rule*. Thus, a "theocracy" is a government ruled by God. Not symbolically or metaphorically, but *actually* ruled by God. As we have seen, Yahweh was *enthroned* in the Holy of Holies, "above the cherubim." Here God does what all kings do: he meets with his people, adjudicates legislative issues, receives tribute, and decrees policy. This means that Israel, from the days of the settlement through the exile, was indeed the kingdom of God on earth.

I find that many Christians are surprised to hear the term "kingdom of God" applied to the Old Testament. Many think this is a New Testament idea. But as Israel was, indeed, "ruled by God" this means that Israel's territory was actually *God's* territory. Because of this, Israel's enemies were *God's* enemies. And Israel's political interests were *God's* political interests. This is an extremely important piece of the theological puzzle when one attempts to understand the nature of the Mosaic Covenant, the monarchy, and how these Old Testament realities relate to the New Testament. Many of the perennially perplexing moral questions that arise between the Old and New Covenants derive from a misunderstanding of this one concept.

So how did God set up his theocratic nation? Deuteronomy 17:14–18:22 tells us that there were three theocratic offices established in the Sinai covenant. Staffed by human representatives, these were the **prophet**, the **priest**, and the **king**. The job description of the priest was to represent the people to God via mediation and sacrifice. The priests maintained and facilitated the cultic system. The prophet spoke for God to the people, essentially as Yahweh's messenger to his vassal nation. Thus, Isaiah, Jeremiah, Ezekiel, and the Twelve received their messages from God as might a diplomat being sent from one head of state to another. The king was the "type man" of the nation. His job was to keep the people of Israel on track in their adherence to the covenant and to live his life as the ideal, covenant-keeping Israelite. As heirs of monarchy, Americans typically assume that out of these three officers, the king was the most powerful. But in Israel's government, this was not the case. In Israel, the human king was only a steward of the true king, Yahweh. It was the prophet (whose job was to speak for the true king) who held the ultimate authority.

In this God-centered government, the priests (all descendants of Levi, Num 3:1–13) ran the central cult site. From Moses onward, there were two levels/castes of priests. The sons of Aaron inherited the first tier—they assisted in sacrifice at the altar, offered oracles and judgment, spoke before the army, and enforced orthodox worship in all its facets. They always served in the central cult site, whether that was at Mount Ebal, Shiloh, or Jerusalem. The Levites, on the other hand, were the second tier. They served throughout the tribes and were on rotation at the central cult site.

Day 1: The Officers

First Contact

When election year rolls around, do you find yourself a bit overwhelmed by all the signs and commercials telling you who you should vote for? I do! And I wind up spending all sorts of time figuring out who everyone is and what they support so that I can best vote responsibly. Why? Because I'm completely acculturated to the idea that I as a citizen should help decide who leads. I've been taught since third grade that an informed citizenry is our government's best chance and I need to do my part. But guess what? The idea that the citizenry had *anything* to do with the choice of who leads was completely foreign to the ancient world. In Israel, offices were either inherited or appointed by God. Unlike the US, there was not an "establishment clause." In Israel there was no separation of church and state. The officers of the state were equally representative of the national faith. Yahweh was king, the law was his word, and prophet, priest, and king were as much representatives of God as they were the government.

Into the Book

Today we take a closer look at what Scripture has to say about the three officers of the theocracy and what they do.

Deuteronomy 17: 14–20

14 When you enter the land the LORD your God is giving you and have taken possession of it and settled in it, and you say, "Let us set a king over us like all the nations around us," 15 be sure to appoint over you a king the LORD your God chooses. He must be from among your fellow Israelites. Do not place a foreigner over you, one who is not an Israelite. 16 The king, moreover, must not acquire great numbers of horses for himself or make the people return to Egypt to get more of them, for the LORD has told you, "You are not to go back that way again." 17 He must not take many wives, or his heart will be led astray. He must not accumulate large amounts of silver and gold.

18 When he takes the throne of his kingdom, he is to write for himself on a scroll a copy of this law, taken from that of the Levitical priests. 19 It is to be with him, and he is to read it all the days of his life so that he may learn to revere the LORD his God and follow carefully all the words of this law 20 and these decrees and not consider himself better than his fellow Israelites and turn from the law to the right or to the left. Then he and his descendants will reign a long time over his kingdom in Israel.

What theocratic office is discussed here?

Highlight the instructions regarding what this officer is to do.

Underline the instructions regarding what he is not to do.

What is the significance of the instructions found in verses 18–20?

Numbers 3:5–10	
[5] The LORD said to Moses, [6] "Bring the tribe of Levi and present them to Aaron the priest to assist him. [7] They are to perform duties for him and for the whole community at the tent of meeting by doing the work of the tabernacle. [8] They are to take care of all the furnishings of the tent of meeting, fulfilling the obligations of the Israelites by doing the work of the tabernacle. [9] Give the Levites to Aaron and his sons; they are the Israelites who are to be given wholly to him. [10] Appoint Aaron and his sons to serve as priests; anyone else who approaches the sanctuary is to be put to death."	What theocratic office is discussed here? Highlight the instructions regarding what this officer is to do. Who does this officer speak for?

Deuteronomy 18:14–20	
[14] The nations you will disposess listen to those who practice sorcery or divination. But as for you, the LORD your God has not permitted you to do so. [15] The LORD your God will raise up for you a prophet like me from among you, from your fellow Israelites. You must listen to him. [16] For this is what you asked of the LORD your God at Horeb on the day of the assemby when you said, "Let us not hear the voice of the LORD our God nor see this great fire anymore, or we will die."	What theocratic office is discussed here?
[17] The LORD said to me: "What they say is good. [18] I will raise up for them a prophet like you from among their fellow Israelites, and I will put my words in his mouth. He will tell them everything I command him. [19] I myself will call to account anyone who does not listen to my words that the prophet speaks in my name. [20] But a prophet who presumes to speak in my name anything I have not commanded, or a prophet who speaks in the name of other gods, is to be put to death."	Highlight the instructions regarding what this officer is to do. Who does this officer speak for?

Real People, Real Places, Real Faith

As we think about our Israelites as real people, we need to ponder how the role of the theocratic officers affected their everyday lives. In Deuteronomy 10:8–9 (cf. 18:1–5) we are told that because of their role in the central sanctuary, "the Levites have no share or inheritance among their fellow Israelites; the Lord is their inheritance, as the LORD your God told them." This is completely unique among the citizenry. Every other Israelite tribe, clan, and family had been given land by which to support themselves. Not the Levites. Their occupation, therefore, was not to farm or fish or craft; their job was to serve the religious needs of the people. As a result, the Levite is regularly listed along with the "widow, orphan, and resident alien" as someone to whom the citizenry should show hospitality and charity. Interesting to me as well is that the Levite was in some sense the "cheerleader" for the army. It was the priest who addressed the army before they would go into battle—not the prophet or the king (see Deut 20:1–4).

As for the prophet, this officer essentially acted as a divine diplomat, bringing the message of the nation's sovereign Yahweh to their steward, the human king. As you noted in your study above, the prophet's job description is fashioned after the role of Moses. God speaks directly to his prophet, and the prophet speaks to the people. If the prophet alters the word he has been given (cf. Deut 13:1–5), he has committed high treason, a capital crime. Keep in mind that in other nations, prophets pretty much told the king what he wanted to hear (in 1 Kings 22:1–28 we see this going on in Israel as well). Thus, being a prophet was not always a popular vocation—people ancient and modern rarely want to hear when they've messed up.

As for the king, in addition to leading the nation in their military and political endeavors, he was to "write for himself on a scroll a copy of this law" and to "read it all the days of his life." Why? Because in Israel, unlike the rest of the ancient Near East, the king was not above the law. "Insider status" did not deliver the king from God's scrutiny. Rather, the king kept a copy of the law "so that he may learn to revere the LORD his God." As Lawson Stone says it: "Kings in Israel were called not to exercise power, create opulent palaces, temples, and capital cities, but to stand as guardians of Yahweh's covenant, upholding the spirit and letter of his moral law. Just as Adam was to tend and guard the garden, the king was to tend and protect the covenant people."[21]

---

[21] Stone, *Judges*, 485.

Our People, Our Places, Our Faith

What would it be like to have the political leaders of your nation subject to God's authority? What if presidents were required to keep a copy of God's moral expectations on their desks at all times, and if they wandered, could expect a visit from the local prophet? A president having an affair called out, in public, by Nathan the prophet (2 Sam 12)! The Secretary of the Environmental Protection Agency confronted by Elijah for stealing an honest man's vineyard (1 Kgs 21)? The United States House Committee on Ethics held accountable for its junior members using their influence to seduce interns and pad their own pockets (1 Sam 2:22–25)? What would our local communities look like if *every* officer of our government played by the same rules, and those rules were God's rules? As my nation is not a theocracy, that will never happen. But what a world it would be if political officials were empowered by divine wisdom and held accountable by divine power? Who would our senators and congressmen be if no one could "buy" a political official with a special interest or deep pockets? Or if elected officials actually planned for the *future* not just the next election? I'm afraid in my nation I will never know. So I comfort myself with the better truth that I am a citizen of another kingdom, I answer to another king, and I look forward to the day when that king returns to his kingdom and sets all things right.

Day 2: The Enthronement

First Contact

What do you picture when you hear the words "coronation day"? Perhaps you picture the crackly newsreels from June 2, 1953 when Queen Elizabeth II became the 39th Sovereign and sixth British queen to be crowned at Westminster Abbey. Or maybe Elsa's coronation in the movie *Frozen* is more your world—a day filled with dancing, feasting, and Anna's exuberant joy? Or perhaps you are like me, and the only king you can see on "coronation day" is Aragorn, son of Arathorn, chieftain of the Dúnedain of Arnor, kneeling before Gandalf the White as the faithful steward of Gondor announces his titles—and the ancient crown of the High King of Gondor is, at last, placed upon his head.

Into the Book

In today's study we'll see what enthronement ceremonies looked like in ancient Israel by looking at Solomon's coronation and comparing that with one of the Psalter's "royal psalms."

Read 1 Kings 1:32–40, 46–48.

> [32] King David said, "Call in Zadok the priest, Nathan the prophet and Benaiah son of Jehoiada." When they came before the king, [33] he said to them: "Take your lord's servants with you and have Solomon my son mount my own mule and take him down to Gihon. [34] There have Zadok the priest and Nathan the prophet anoint him king over Israel. Blow the trumpet and shout, 'Long live King Solomon!' [35] Then you are to go up with him, and he is to come and sit on my throne and reign in my place. I have appointed him ruler over Israel and Judah."
>
> [36] Benaiah son of Jehoiada answered the king, "Amen! May the Lord, the God of my lord the king, so declare it. [37] As the Lord was with my lord the king, so may he be with Solomon to make his throne even greater than the throne of my lord King David!"

 [38] So Zadok the priest, Nathan the prophet, Benaiah son of Jehoiada, the Kerethites and the Pelethites went down and had Solomon mount King David's mule, and they escorted him to Gihon. [39] Zadok the priest took the horn of oil from the sacred tent and anointed Solomon. Then they sounded the trumpet and all the people shouted, "Long live King Solomon!" [40] And all the people went up after him, playing pipes and rejoicing greatly, so that the ground shook with the sound.

 [46] "Moreover, Solomon has taken his seat on the royal throne. [47] Also, the royal officials have come to congratulate our lord King David, saying, 'May your God make Solomon's name more famous than yours and his throne greater than yours!' And the king bowed in worship on his bed [48] and said, 'Praise be to the Lord, the God of Israel, who has allowed my eyes to see a successor on my throne today.'"

○ Who did David call for to anoint Solomon as king?

○ With what was Solomon anointed?

○ What happened after Solomon was anointed?

○ Where did Solomon take his seat?

Now read Psalm 2. As you do, look for similarities with the 1 Kings passage above.

○ Who does "his anointed" refer to?

○ Where does the king take his seat?

○ Who placed him there?

Psalm 2

¹ Why do the nations conspire
     and the peoples plot in vain?
² The kings of the earth rise up
     and the rulers band together
          against the LORD and against his anointed,
               saying,
³ "Let us break their chains
     and throw off their shackles."
⁴ The One enthroned in heaven laughs;
     the LORD scoffs at them.
⁵ He rebukes them in his anger
     and terrifies them in his wrath, saying,
⁶ "I have installed my king
     on Zion, my holy mountain."
⁷ I will proclaim the LORD's decree:
He said to me, "You are my son;
     today I have become your father.

⁸ Ask me,
     and I will make the nations your
          inheritance,
     the ends of the earth your
          possession.
⁹ You will break them with a rod of iron;
     you will dash them to pieces like pottery."
¹⁰ Therefore, you kings, be wise;
     be warned, you rulers of the earth.
¹¹ Serve the LORD with fear
     and celebrate his rule with trembling.
¹² Kiss his son, or he will be angry
     and your way will lead to your destruction,
for his wrath can flare up in a moment.
     Blessed are all who take refuge in him.

Real People, Real Places, Real Faith

In the narrative of 1 Samuel 16:1–13 we read that Yahweh instructed the prophet Samuel to go to Jesse of Bethlehem because Yahweh had "rejected [Saul] as king over Israel" and had "chosen one of [Jesse's] sons to be king" (v. 1). Samuel was to anoint the one whom Yahweh indicated. One by one Jesse's sons come forward, and Yahweh rejects all of them until David is brought before him. Then Yahweh says, "Rise and anoint him; this is the one" (v. 12). David was Yahweh's divine choice.

This idea of divine choice of the king is evident throughout the ancient Near East.[22] In Mesopotamia (the nations of Sumer, Babylonia, and Assyria), it was expected that the deity chose his or her ruler. One familiar example is King Hammurabi of Babylonia (ca. 1792–1750 BCE). You have likely heard of his famous law code. He speaks of his coronation day as that day "When Shamash . . . with radiant face had joyfully looked

Wooden statue of Pharoah Senusret I (ruled 1918-1875 BCE) holding a shepherd's staff (the "Heka") an internationally recognized symbol of leadership.

upon me—me, his favorite shepherd, Hammurabi."[23] As I'm sure you noticed, and we will discuss further in the Shepherd's psalm (Psalm 23), Hammurabi speaks of himself as "shepherd." (Indeed, the symbol of a shepherd's staff as the symbol of leadership was so embedded in the mind of the ancients that this became the symbol for "ruler" in Egyptian hieroglyphs!). First Chronicles 28:6 reiterates this shared worldview when it speaks of Yahweh's choice of Solomon: "I have chosen him to be my son, and I will be his father." So the identity of Israel's human king was always subject to Yahweh's will. Yahweh was the suzerain, the human king the vassal. Any human king who grew foggy on this concept would find himself looking at his replacement.

---

22   DeVaux, *Ancient Israel: Its Life and Institutions*, 100.
23   Frankfort, *Kingship and the Gods*, 238.

Our People, Our Places, Our Faith

As we ponder God's choice of Solomon as David's replacement, we who know the backstory of this choice should be a bit taken aback. Solomon is the child of Bathsheba. Bathsheba, as Matthew 1:6 continues to remind us, was Uriah's wife. Of all the blunders David made in his life, this is the blunder that gets the most press. It is also the one that seems to have had the most consequences. What were the consequences of David's sin? The list is long. The fact that David summoned another man's wife for sex and then disposed of her as though she were nothing is the beginning. The fact that he dragged Joab into his conspiracy to murder her husband is the middle. The fact that Uriah dies so unjustly, as a righteous man who was faithfully serving his king, might be the end. But the compromise and trauma that David inflicted on Bathsheba will continue to stalk David's steps. Their first child dies, despite David's desperate outcry to God to forgive him and spare the child (2 Sam 12). Next, we learn of further sexual misconduct in David's house when Amnon ambushes and rapes his sister Tamar (2 Sam 13). Her full brother Absalom, watching his father and sovereign do nothing, is first enraged and then disillusioned, and begins to plot his own revenge. The end result will be a fractured household—a son dead (2 Sam 13), a daughter destroyed, an attempted coup (2 Sam 18), and yet another son dead. And in the center of it? David's sin. What can be done? "But God . . ." as my prayer partners would say. But God redeems this shattered scenario and chooses Bathsheba's second son as heir. Solomon, whose name means "peace" (it comes from *shalom*) is set over David's kingdom. And as the historians will tell us, the era of Solomon as described in 2 Kings is the most prosperous and powerful of Israel's monarchy. This united kingdom controls more territory and knows more financial success than any other era in Israel's history. The finances were such that the temple was built, strategic cities fortified, and international trade established possibly as far as India. Can God redeem our mistakes? Our crimes and rebellion? Can he make up for the years the locust has eaten away? Yes, yes he can.

Day 3: The Protection

First Contact

What is your favorite war movie? In my household, you can predict the gender gap by who wants to watch *Saving Private Ryan* or *Glory* and who doesn't. And I'm sure you can guess which side my husband lands on and which I land on. But even though I don't typically enjoy watching things (or God help us, people) blow up, there are still aspects of the best of these films that capture me every time. The leading example being the courage and character of soldiers who are willing to put their lives on the line to protect the things they love. The band of brothers that compels an enlisted man or woman to run back *into* the fray because they simply will not leave a comrade behind. The fortitude that sent the all-Black 54th Massachusetts Infantry Regiment forward into certain death at the Second Battle of Fort Wagner for a country that did not even recognize them as fully human *(Glory)*. Although as a historian I am well aware that all war is hell. And although I cry my way through most of these films and do the same on Veteran's Day, the dignity of these men and women who "stand on a wall" for the sake of their country deeply inspires me every time.

Into the Book

If you've worked through some of the other *Epic of Eden* studies then you'll recall that the relationship between Yahweh and Israel in the Mosaic covenant is a suzerain/vassal relationship: Yahweh is the suzerain and Israel is the vassal. As such, Yahweh promises military protection to his vassal. Thus, when you read through Psalms you will hear a lot of talk about the political enemies of the kingdom, the cry for deliverance from these enemies, and even the pleas of the people for their enemies to suffer.

Read (most of) Psalm 18. It's a long one!

○ Why did David cry to Yahweh? Place brackets around the section of verses that describe his situation and need for help.

○ How did Yahweh respond? Place a box around the section of verses that describe his response. (You may want to choose one color to box what he did to David's enemies and one color to box what he did for David.)

○ <u>Underline</u> the reasons David provides for Yahweh's actions toward him.

○ In verses 32–36 place <u>dotted lines</u> under the ways in which Yahweh prepares David for battle.

○ Highlight all the verbs in verses 37–43. Choose one color for the verbs describing what David did and one color for the verbs describing what Yahweh did.

○ Finally, notice how David begins and ends the psalm.

Psalm 18

A psalm of David the servant of the Lord.
He sang to the Lord the words of this song
when the Lord delivered him from the hand
of all of his enemies and from the hand of
Saul. He said:

¹ I love you, LORD, my strength.

² The LORD is my rock, my fortress and my
    deliverer;
  my God is my rock, in whom I take refuge,
  my shield and the horn of my salvation, my
    stronghold.

³ I called to the LORD, who is worthy of praise,
  and I have been saved from my enemies.

⁴ The cords of death entangled me;
    the torrents of destruction overwhelmed
      me.
⁵ The cords of the grave coiled around me;
    the snares of death confronted me.

⁶ In my distress I called to the LORD;
    I cried to my God for help.
  From his temple he heard my voice;
    my cry came before him, into his ears.

⁷ The earth trembled and quaked,
    and the foundations of the mountains
      shook;
    they trembled because he was angry.
⁸ Smoke rose from his nostrils;
consuming fire came from his mouth,
    burning coals blazed out of it.
⁹ He parted the heavens and came down;
    dark clouds were under his feet.
¹⁰ He mounted the cherubim and flew;
    he soared on the wings of the wind.
¹¹ He made darkness his covering, his canopy
      around him—
    the dark rain clouds of the sky.
¹² Out of the brightness of his presence clouds
      advanced,
    with hailstones and bolts of lightning.
¹³ The LORD thundered from heaven;
    the voice of the Most High resounded.
¹⁴ He shot his arrows and scattered the enemy,
    with great bolts of lightning he routed
      them.
¹⁵ The valleys of the sea were exposed
    and the foundations of the earth laid bare
    at your rebuke, LORD,
    at the blast of breath from your nostrils.

¹⁶ He reached down from on high and took
      hold of me;
    he drew me out of deep waters.
¹⁷ He rescued me from my powerful enemy,
from my foes, who were too strong for me.
¹⁸ They confronted me in the day of
      my disaster,
    but the LORD was my support.
¹⁹ He brought me out into a spacious place;
    he rescued me because he delighted in me.

²⁰ The LORD has dealt with me according to my
      righteousness;
    according to the cleanness of my hands he
      has rewarded me.
²¹ For I have kept the ways of the LORD;
    I am not guilty of turning from my God.
²² All his laws are before me;
    I have not turned away from his decrees.
²³ I have been blameless before him
    and have kept myself from sin.
²⁴ The LORD has rewarded me according to my
      righteousness,
    according to the cleanness of my hands in
      his sight.

²⁵ To the faithful you show yourself faithful,
    to the blameless you show yourself
      blameless,
²⁶ to the pure you show yourself pure,
    but to the devious you show yourself
      shrewd.
²⁷ You save the humble
    but bring low those whose eyes are
      haughty.

²⁸ You, LORD, keep my lamp burning;
    my God turns my darkness into light.
²⁹ With your help I can advance against a troop;
    with my God I can scale a wall.

³⁰ As for God, his way is perfect:
    The LORD's word is flawless;
    he shields all who take refuge in him.
³¹ For who is God besides the LORD?
    And who is the Rock except our God?
³² It is God who arms me with strength
    and keeps my way secure.
³³ He makes my feet like the feet of a deer;
    he causes me to stand on the heights.
³⁴ He trains my hands for battle;
    my arms can bend a bow of bronze.
³⁵ You make your saving help my shield,
    and your right hand sustains me;
    your help has made me great.
³⁶ You provide a broad path for my feet,
    so that my ankles do not give way.

³⁷ I pursued my enemies and overtook them;
    I did not turn back till they were
    destroyed.
³⁸ I crushed them so that they could not rise;
    they fell beneath my feet.
³⁹ You armed me with strength for battle;
    you humbled my adversaries before me.
⁴⁰ You made my enemies turn their backs in
    flight,

and I destroyed my foes.
⁴¹ They cried for help, but there was no one to
    save them—
    to the LORD, but he did not answer.
⁴² I beat them as fine as windblown dust;
    I trampled them like mud in the streets.
⁴³ You have delivered me from the attacks of
    the people;
    you have made me the head of nations.
People I did not know now serve me,
⁴⁴   foreigners cower before me;
    as soon as they hear of me, they obey me.
⁴⁵ They all lose heart;
    they come trembling from their
    strongholds.

⁴⁶ The LORD lives! Praise be to my Rock!
    Exalted be God my Savior!
⁴⁷ He is the God who avenges me,
    who subdues nations under me,
⁴⁸   who saves me from my enemies.
You exalted me above my foes;
    from a violent man you rescued me.
⁴⁹ Therefore I will praise you, LORD, among the
    nations;
    I will sing the praises of your name.

⁵⁰ He gives his king great victories;
    he shows unfailing love to his anointed,
    to David and to his descendants forever.

Real People, Real Places, Real Faith

If you've read through the book of Judges or the books of 1 and 2 Kings, you've no doubt noticed how often the biblical narrators speak of armies, battles, wars, and weapons. You've come across military words such as *siege, fortified walls, battering rams*, and more. In fact, the word translated warfare occurs over 300 times in the Old Testament!

So, what did ancient warfare look like? Obviously no fighter jets or machine guns. Rather, the most common form of armed conflict was hand-to-hand combat using short-range weapons, which would include things like clubs, axes, spears, daggers, and swords. Perhaps one of the most well-known sword stories in the Bible is that of Ehud found in Judges 3:12–23. Here, Ehud, a left-handed man, was able to hide his "short sword" under his clothing, walk into a private audience with King Eglon of Moab, and assassinate the king in his own chamber. Medium-range weapons included spears and javelins used for thrusting and throwing. The sling and slingstone were commonly used long-range weapons. In fact, in the battle of David and Goliath, one reason that David had a chance is that he brought a long-range weapon. If David had ever gotten within reach, Goliath would have had him for lunch. But his sling allowed our underdog to keep his distance.

It was the introduction of the chariot that made the other long-range weapon—the bow and arrow—effective on the battlefield. Chariots are often described as "mobile archery platforms" as they made it possible for archers to participate in field encounters as opposed to being stationary defenders of fortified cities. A skilled archer could shoot an arrow over 200 meters: a slinger could propel a stone up to 150 miles an hour! Not only does the biblical text provide information about archers and slingers (for example, see 1 Kgs 22:29–38; 1 Sam 17:1–51), but Assyrian reliefs provide detailed images of these highly-skilled and coveted military specialists.

In the book of Kings we read several times how either the Assyrians or the Babylonians "laid siege" to cities in Israel (for example, see 2 Kgs 17; 24; 25). Siege warfare, perfected by the Assyrians, was used for sustained attacks on walled (fortified) cities. The invading army would set up camp outside the city cutting off the city's food and water supplies. Ramps were built to facilitate siege engines and battering rams in order to breach the wall. We have many depictions of this fearsome form of warfare, not the least being the Assyrian reliefs commemorating their successful siege on the Judean city of Lachish in 701 BCE.

Our People, Our Places, Our Faith

Twenty-first-century America is not as comfortable as it once was with the realities of soldiering. Unlike my father's day, enlisting in the military is no longer recognized as "romantic" or "noble." Perhaps America has seen too many wars. Or perhaps we have gone unthreatened for so long that we view ourselves as impregnable and our military as superfluous. However this shift of worldview has come about, many have grown uncomfortable with the images and metaphors of war. But images of war permeate the book of Psalms.

So how do we in the New Covenant era translate the battle images of the Psalms into our current context? As stated a number of times in this study, your nation/my nation are no longer theocracies. Yahweh reigns from heaven (not the temple), and the citizens of the kingdom of God may be found in every political entity on earth. Therefore, the "kingdom of God" is no longer a single nation, and there are no longer national boundaries to defend in the name of God. Moreover, we the community of faith no longer go to war to extend the boundaries of this kingdom. Rather, according to Paul,

> [3] For though we live in the world, we do not wage war as the world does. [4] The weapons we fight with are not the weapons of the world. On the contrary, they have divine power to demolish strongholds. [5] We demolish arguments and every pretension that sets itself up against the knowledge of God, and we take captive every thought to make it obedient to Christ. (2 Cor 10:3–5)

In other words, yes, the battle against evil continues. But in this new covenant, our opponent is no longer the military force of another nation. Rather, our opponents are the forces of evil that have targeted the kingdom of God. Therefore, Paul exhorts us:

> [10] Finally, be strong in the Lord and in his mighty power. [11] Put on the **full armor** of God, so that you can take your stand against the devil's **schemes**. [12] For our **struggle** is not against flesh and blood, but against the rulers, against the authorities, against the powers of this dark world and against the **spiritual forces** of evil in the heavenly realms. [13] Therefore put on the **full armor** of God, so that when the day of evil comes, you may be able to **stand your ground**, and after you have done everything, to **stand**. [14] Stand firm then, with the **belt of truth** buckled around your waist, with the **breastplate** of righteousness in place, [15] and with your feet fitted with the readiness that comes from the gospel of peace. [16] In addition to all this, take up the **shield** of faith,

with which you can extinguish all the **flaming arrows** of the evil one. [17] Take the **helmet** of salvation and the **sword** of the Spirit, which is the word of God.

[18] And pray in the Spirit on all occasions with all kinds of prayers and requests. With this in mind, be **alert** and always keep on praying for all the Lord's people. [19] Pray also for me, that whenever I speak, words may be given me so that I will **fearlessly** make known the mystery of the gospel. (Eph 6:10–19; boldface is my own)

How do we translate the words of the psalmist into our world? The battle continues. But our enemy is no longer Edom or Babylonia or the Amalekites. The kingdom is still vulnerable, and we can never drop our guard. No, we must be trained and ready. But this time we are ready with orthodoxy, prayer, and confidence in our king who leads us. Indeed, "He trains my hands for battle; my arms can bend a bow of bronze. You make your saving help my shield, and your right hand sustains me; your help has made me great" (Ps 18:34–35).

Day 4: A Psalm

First Contact

If I were to ask you right now what is stirring up fear and worry, what would it be? What anxiety is demanding your attention as you attempt to focus on this study? Is it a situation at work? Slander from an enemy (or worse, from a friend)? Is it a diagnosis you are waiting for or bills that are impossible to pay? A friend who has gone silent and you're waiting for the fallout? Are you worried about your child? It is interesting to me that as I read the Psalms I am constantly reading of people who need protection, support, and deliverance. Yet I live among a community of faith who seems to think that bad things shouldn't happen to good people. So here's the news flash—bad things do happen to good people. All the time. And just because something bad is happening, it does not mean that God has abandoned you. Rather, it means he is waiting to *help* you.

Read through Psalm 72 once (preferably out loud) without stopping to take notes. Then follow the instructions in Reading & Observing in your second reading.

Psalm 72
Of Solomon

1 Endow the king with your justice, O God,
the royal son with your righteousness.
2 May he judge your people in righteousness,
your afflicted ones with justice.

3 May the mountains bring prosperity to the
people,
the hills the fruit of righteousness.
4 May he defend the afflicted among the people
and save the children of the needy;
may he crush the oppressor.
5 May he endure as long as the sun,
as long as the moon, through all
generations.
6 May he be like rain falling on a mown field,
like showers watering the earth.
7 In his days may the righteous flourish
and prosperity abound till the moon is no
more.

8 May he rule from sea to sea
and from the River to the ends of
the earth.
9 May the desert tribes bow before him
and his enemies lick the dust.

10 May the kings of Tarshish and of distant shores
bring tribute to him.
May the kings of Sheba and Seba
present him gifts.
11 May all kings bow down to him
and all nations serve him.

12 For he will deliver the needy who cry out,
the afflicted who have no one to help.
13 He will take pity on the weak and the needy
and save the needy from death.
14 He will rescue them from oppression and
violence,
for precious is their blood in his sight.

15 Long may he live!
May gold from Sheba be given him.
May people ever pray for him
and bless him all day long.
16 May grain abound throughout the land;
on the tops of the hills may it sway.
May the crops flourish like Lebanon
and thrive like the grass of the field.
17 May his name endure forever;
may it continue as long as the sun.

Then all nations will be blessed through him,
and they will call him blessed.

[18] Praise be to the LORD God, the God of Israel,
who alone does marvelous deeds.
[19] Praise be to his glorious name forever;
may the whole earth be filled with
his glory.

Amen and Amen.

[20] This concludes the prayers of David son of Jesse.

Reading & Observing

Read through the psalm again, this time looking for these things:

○ Which collection does the psalm belong to (Book I, II, III, IV, V)?

○ Is there a superscript? If so, what is it? Who is the psalm attributed to?

○ What type of psalm is it? (What is the psalmist doing: praying, praising, complaining, giving thanks, etc.?)

○ Who is the psalmist praying for in this psalm?

○ What does the psalmist request? Place a bracket around the verses that contain the psalmist's requests.

○ What verses describe what the king will do and for whom? Place a different colored set of brackets around those verses.

○ How does the psalmist end this prayer?

Responding

We opened today's study with the question of what is stirring up fear and worry in you? Remember that God has not abandoned you . . . he is waiting to help you. As Psalm 72 reminds us, "He will deliver the needy who cry out" (v. 12). How do you respond? Choose one (or more) of the following as a response to your study of this psalm.

○ Sing the psalm! Go to **http://psalms.seedbed.com/** and navigate your way to Psalm 72. Choose one (or all) of the tune options there and sing this psalm to the Lord.

○ Illustrate the psalm! For those of you who are artistically inclined you might be interested in an ancient and beautiful tradition known as "illuminated manuscripts." There are pages set aside at the back of the book (pages 209–217) for you to create your own illuminated psalms as well as a sample to get your creative juices flowing.

○ Pray the psalm! Put in your own names and places, and let the ancients pray with you!

○ Choose one paragraph of this psalm to memorize.

○ Set this psalm to your own music. Let the words find their way into your heart.

Tips to Memorizing
  ○ Start small
  ○ Write it down
  ○ Say it out loud
  ○ Repeat

SESSION 4

Interpreting the Psalms: Theocracy

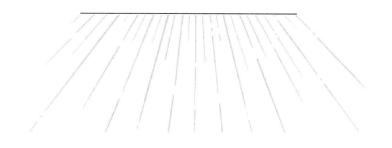

SESSION 4: GROUP MEETING

Schedule

GROUP MEETING
Session 4 Video Teaching and Discussion

INDIVIDUAL STUDY
Day 1: The Lens-Setter
Day 2: The Worship
Day 3: The Power
Day 4: A Psalm

Debrief & Discover

Ask your group members to list three differences between theocracy and democracy.

Watch Session 4 Video:
INTERPRETING THE PSALMS: THEOCRACY
(26 minutes)

Video Notes

These are provided for you and your group members to follow along during the video as well as to offer room for note taking (writing down questions and aha moments as you like).

I.   What is a theocracy?

    A. theos + *kratos* (< kratew) = a government ruled by God

    B. Theocratic offices (Deut 16:18–18:22; Exod 19–23)

        1. Prophet: speaks for God to the people

        2. Priest: speaks for the people to God

        3. King: political leader, supposed to keep the nation on track in its adherence to the covenant

    C. The Kingdom of God in the Old Covenant . . .

        1. . . . was the ancient political entity known as the nation of Israel

       2.   . . . had political boundaries

       3.   . . . had an army

II.   Theocracy in the book of Psalms

   A. Theocracy in Psalm 2

   B. God in the temple (Pss 84:1–4; 95:1–2; 100:4)

   C. Israel and Judah: citizens of the kingdom of God; all others are not (Pss 97:7–9; 59:5; 99:1–2)

   D. Priests and sacrifice

       1.   Care for the holy place

       2.   Administrate the task of sacrifice

       3.   Priest vs. Levite

   E. The king and his battles (Pss 18:32–38; 27:3; 137:7–9)

   F. Israel's political enemies (Ps 76:1–6)

III.   The New Covenant

  A. Not a theocracy

  B. The people of God no longer just the citizens of Israel

  C. The place of God no longer simply Canaan

  D. The presence of God no longer just the tabernacle

Dialogue, Digest & Do

○ How does the "kingdom of God" in ancient Israel differ from the "kingdom of God" in the New Covenant?

○ Discuss the ways in which Israel's system of sacrifice differed from those in the rest of the ancient Near East.

○ Sandy says that the Psalms are much more about the experience of the worshiper than didactics; experience over theology is the emphasis. How does understanding this affect your reading and understanding of the Psalms?

○ Have you ever felt you couldn't express your real emotion to God? Why? What do you think about that now?

As discussed above, the Psalms are much more about the experience of the worshiper than theology. In the Psalms we hear the hurt, rage, and anger of the ancient Israelites. Have you ever allowed yourself to truly express your emotions to God? Good news . . . God can handle our emotions, even when those emotions include outrage, anger, and hurt.

In your bonus psalms studies, you've been challenged, of responding, to memorize one paragraph of the psalm under study. Has anyone chosen that option? How is the memorization going?

Next Week

In addition to sacred space and theocracy, there is yet one more thing we need to understand in order to properly interpret the book of Psalms. We'll explore that topic next week.

Closing Prayer

Ask your group members if there is anything they would like prayer for—especially something highlighted by this week's video. Are you keeping a list yet?

Reminder: If you are behind in the reading, pick up with the individual study tomorrow to get back on track.

SESSION 4: INDIVIDUAL STUDY

The Power of Poetry

A Word from Sandy

I must confess that I am not a person who sits out on my back patio sipping tea and reading poetry. And I'm afraid that my idea of a long winter's night does not typically involve Lord Byron. But that doesn't change the fact that lyric, elevated speech, and poetry touch me in a way that prose cannot. As a result, when I hear the Gettysburg address recited aloud, I am transfixed. When in the course of teaching I rehearse Martin Luther King's "I Have a Dream," I find myself choking back tears. I have yet to read Isaiah 53 without completely losing it. Why? Because "high eloquence" sneaks past my barriers and lays siege to my soul. When words and ideas are presented through poetry and song, they are no longer "out there." They are "in here," and they *demand* my response.

Real Time & Space

As we approach the book of Psalms we need to know what *sort* of literature we are approaching. Identifying genre is always the first step in good biblical interpretation. You don't read a letter from your mother the same way you read the instruction manual for your new dishwasher. You don't watch the *David Letterman Show* or *Oprah* with the same expectations as you do a network news program (or at least you shouldn't!). As a native audience, you know this instinctively. As a non-native reader of Hebrew literature, it is possible that you don't know this. So as we approach the Psalms, let's get our categories straight.

In our video session this week, I will describe the book of Psalms as *poetry* (which focuses on the *experience* of the individual worshiper) rather than *didactics*. "Didactics" is a knowledge-based approach to education—it champions information, theory, and objectivity. The instruction manual for your new dishwasher would have similar objectives. In the Old Testament, the book of Proverbs would be a good example of the didactic method; Deuteronomy would be another. In the New Testament, the books of Romans and

Galatians are also great examples. These books have as their primary objective to *teach* the reader. The book of Psalms, however, does not. Rather, the book of Psalms is a collection of poetic expressions of a worshiper's celebration, grief, anger, gratitude, doubt, and belief. Although the psalmist is presupposing and expressing doctrine (remember Psalm 1, our Torah psalm), the objective of the author is prayer and worship, not necessarily instruction. We do have some "didactic poetry" (poems designed to instruct) in the Psalter—Psalms 1; 19:7–14; 32; 34; 73; 112; 119; 127; 128; and 133 have been categorized this way—but the bulk of our psalms champion experience, response, and emotion.

And what about the Psalter as *poetry?* As we will discuss in this session, poetry can be defined as "[a] complex of heightening effects used in combinations and intensities that vary widely from composition to composition . . . that marks the language as 'special.'"[24] Some poetry is highly structured (for example, a sonnet or a haiku), some is much more free-flowing (for example, e e cummings). But all poetry "strangefies." Poetry "strangefies" by reversing and undermining standard syntax; personifying inanimate objects or ideas; and using hyperbole, metaphor, and jarring word pairs. What is the objective? To move and to persuade. In the Psalms, sometimes the target of persuasion is God himself; sometimes it is the reader or the listening congregation.

Any community's poetry is highly acculturated. In other words, what constitutes poetry is specific to the community for whom it is written. As James Kugel, Starr Professor of Hebrew Literature at Harvard University says in his highly influential book, *The Idea of Biblical Poetry*, the core concept of Israelite poetry is "the seconding sentence."[25] *Repetition* is the stuff of biblical poetry. Whereas in American and European poetry *rhyme* is expected, in Hebrew *repetition* is what creates high eloquence. The repetition can come in diads or triads, synonymous or antithetical, chiastic or ring compositions—the poet is the artist and can compose at will.

A and as a matter of fact B
  A and even more so B
    A and in contrast B

The clauses that create "seconding" will be terse, roughly equal in length, and distributed throughout the piece in any fashion the artist deems beautiful. Essentially, what we have in Hebrew poetry is a *rhythm of sense.*

---

[24] Kugel, *The Idea of Biblical Poetry*, 94.
[25] Kugel, 1.

Day 1: The Lens-Setter

First Contact

I am not a morning person. I often see the dawn . . . but it's from the other side. As a result, when I am keeping the internationally acclaimed schedule of "early to bed and early to rise," I need some help to get the day rolling. Caffeine is essential. So is music. I not only need to shake my gray matter loose of slumber, but I need help setting my lens for the day. I need someone to rehearse to me what God's will is—his good, pleasing and perfect will" (Rom 12:2). I need to be reminded that God is sovereign, that "this world in its present form is passing away" (1 Cor 7:31), and that God is for me (Ps 124:1). And so to my family's chagrin, I play praise music *loud* . . . a lot. Why? I'm setting my lens. I'm reminding myself of the kingdom I cannot see. I am admonishing my soul: "Because the Sovereign Lord helps me, I will not be disgraced. Therefore have I set my face like flint, and I know I will not be put to shame" (Isa 50:7).

Into the Book

Read Psalm 1 on the following page. As you read, use the following to engage with the psalm.

- ○ What figures of speech do you see?

- ○ Underline two examples of simile.

- ○ Circle three instances of repetition. (Take a look back at Real Time and Space regarding Hebrew repetition. See an example in verse 1 below.)

- ○ Place boxes around two contrasts.

Psalm 1

¹ Blessed is the one

    who does not walk in step with the wicked

or stand in the way that sinners take

    or sit in the company of mockers

² but whose delight is in the law of the Lord,

    and who meditates on his law day

    and night.

³ That person is like a tree planted by streams

    of water,

which yields its fruit in season

and whose leaf does not wither—

whatever they do prospers.

⁴ Not so the wicked!

    They are like chaff

    that the wind blows away.

⁵ Therefore the wicked will not stand in the

    judgment,

    nor sinners in the assembly of the

    righteous.

⁶ For the Lord watches over the way of the

    righteous,

    but the way of the wicked leads to

    destruction.

Real People, Real Places, Real Faith

As we discussed a few lessons ago, Psalm 1 is a "Torah psalm," meaning that it celebrates the role of the Torah in the life of the faithful Israelite. As we discussed, this psalm is placed at the forefront of the collection because it is intended to serve as a "lens-setter." The one who reads the Psalms must read the book knowing that the faith described and expressed here is built upon the declarations of the Torah.

As we move through the Psalms we hear all sorts of emotion and particularities regarding the perceived need of the author. We read of melodies and instruments, liturgists and congregational responses, holidays and life events that must be celebrated. Do we find our worshipers sometimes frightened? Angry? Overflowing with giddiness from an impossiblity that just became possible? Yes. Are they busy with staff and programs, outreach and organization, building and expansion? Yes.

The topics and events shift regularly. But one thing does not shift—that is the shared orthodoxy of the participants. The posture of your Bible and your inherited faith is always the same: orthodoxy is a nonnegotiable. This is why the king must have a copy of the Torah on hand as he carries out his royal duties; this is why the prophet is warned in Deuteronomy 13:1–5 that regardless of how impressive his miracles might be, if he strays from the covenant, he is to be executed as a false prophet. This is why the Levites "belong to Yahweh"—they stand directly responsible to God for the tasks of congregational service they carry out. And this is why the community of faith cannot simply pursue what "seems right" or "feels good" in their faith or their worship practices. There is *content* to the Christian faith. And orthodoxy is nonnegotiable.

Our People, Our Places, Our Faith

Back in the first individual study we discussed one of my pet peeves: "Jesus or My Boyfriend Songs." One of the things that drives me crazy about this sort of "worship" music is that the lyrics are so shallow. Rather than challenging the community of faith to be who it is called to be, rehearsing the mighty acts of God, or declaring the character and wisdom of God against whatever is in vogue that week, these songs simply tell us what we want to hear. And of course they tell us what we want to hear with very holy sounding words, majestic orchestration, killer percussion, and super-attractive worship leaders. Kind of like 2 Timothy 4:3: "For the time will come when men will not put up with sound doctrine. Instead, to suit their own desires, they will gather around them a great number of teachers to say what their itching ears want to hear." I first memorized this passage from the NASB which translates "wanting to have their ears tickled, they will accumulate for themselves teachers in accordance with their own desires." The idea of "tickling" really catches my attention. Because I, like many of you, am attracted to particular worship songs for all sorts of reasons beyond the lyrics—the cadence, presentation, bridge, harmony, composition, and the like. And as a result I might just be willing to overlook its *content*.

But Psalm 1 has already taught us that the law of God is the source and the foundation of our worship as a community. Orthodoxy is a nonnegotiable. It doesn't matter how "pretty" some aspect of public worship might be, or even how socially endorsed. If it compromises the unique salvific effect of Jesus, it's out of there. If it encourages the community of faith to stray, get it gone. If it focuses on how good we look, as opposed to how good God looks? Think twice.

Day 2: The Worship

First Contact

Have you ever been at a church service and found yourself wondering if the person leading worship was more concerned with their hair and outfit than actual worship? Or perhaps wondered if the real investment up front was showcasing the quality of the vocals (or instrumentation) rather than leading the community of faith into an encounter with the living God? Have you ever sat in a congregation and felt like a spectator at a totally hype concert as opposed to a participant in a worship service? Or perhaps the opposite, realized that the people around you singing about joy and power and transformation looked absolutely miserable? Hmmm . . . what's the deal with that?

Into the Book

In the days of the prophet Isaiah, God was not at all happy with "business as usual" in Israelite worship. And so he sent his man Isaiah to the crowds gathered at the temple for "worship," and this is what he had to say in Isaiah 1:10–17:

Isaiah 1:10–17

¹⁰ Hear the word of the LORD,
  you rulers of Sodom;
listen to the instruction of our God,
  you people of Gomorrah!
¹¹ "The multitude of your sacrifices—
  what are they to me?" says the LORD.
"I have more than enough of burnt offerings,
  of rams and the fat of fattened animals;
I have no pleasure
  in the blood of bulls and lambs and goats.
¹² When you come to appear before me,
  who has asked this of you,
  this trampling of my courts?
¹³ Stop bringing meaningless offerings!
  Your incense is detestable to me.
New Moons, Sabbaths and convocations—
  I cannot bear your worthless assemblies.

¹⁴ Your New Moon feasts and your appointed
    festivals
  I hate with all my being.
They have become a burden to me;
  I am weary of bearing them.
¹⁵ When you spread out your hands in prayer,
  I hide my eyes from you;
even when you offer many prayers,
  I am not listening.
Your hands are full of blood!

¹⁶ Wash and make yourselves clean.
  Take your evil deeds out of my sight;
  stop doing wrong.
¹⁷ Learn to do right; seek justice.
  Defend the oppressed.
Take up the cause of the fatherless;
  plead the case of the widow.

❍ How does Isaiah address his audience in verse 10? Why do you think he chooses these names? (See Gen 18–19.)

❍ Circle the adjectives God uses to describe Israel's sacrifices, offerings, and assemblies.

❍ Underline the phrases God uses to express his attitude toward Israel's worship and the worshipers (i.e., phrases that begin with "I . . .").

❍ Highlight the reason why God was not listening to their prayers or receiving their sacrifices (which were all orthodox, legitimate expressions of worship).

❍ Place boxes around the commands God gives the people. What did he want from them?

99

Real People, Real Places, Real Faith

As you learned above, all the expressions of worship at the Jerusalem temple named in the Isaiah passage were *legitimate* expressions of Israelite worship—nothing in this mix is somehow pagan or heretical. But still Yahweh is disgusted by it. How can that be? Well, as the passage communicates pretty clearly, these people were in some fashion "going through the motions." They were carrying out the actions of worship (showing up on time, singing the songs, bowing their heads during prayer, dropping money in the plate, etc.), but their hearts were far away. More importantly, their daily behavior was far away.

The people of Isaiah's day were showing up at regularly scheduled worship services, bringing all the right sacrifices and singing all the right songs, but *living* like heathens. Specifically, they were ignoring the heart of God while still attempting to identify as belonging to God. And God was not amused. "Your hands are full of blood!" Yahweh declares: "Seek justice. Defend the oppressed. Take up the cause of the fatherless; plead the case of the widow!" So God not only refused to accept their worship, he sent his messenger to confront the compromise. The prophet Amos had similar words for the northern kingdom when he was called to confront their compromise. Hear his message as paraphrased in *The Message:*

> I can't stand your religious meetings.
>> I'm fed up with your conferences and conventions.
> I want nothing to do with your religion projects,
>> your pretentious slogans and goals.
> I'm sick of your fund-raising schemes,
>> your public relations and image making
> I've had all I can take of your noisy ego-music.
>> When was the last time you sang to *me?*
> Do you know what I want?
>> I want justice—oceans of it.
> I want fairness—rivers of it.
>> That's what I want. That's *all* I want. (Amos 5:21–24 MSG)

Can you see *us* in this call-out? "When was the last time you sang to *me?*" Yahweh asks. When was the last time your church truly made *God* the focus of a worship service? Not the elegant sanctuary and precisely executed exchange of platform responsibilities. Not the captivatingly edgy worship band complete with lights, ambiance, and animated wallpaper backgrounds for slides. Not "the experience" of the congregation or the professionalism of the preacher. As Samuel Terrien has taught us: "A service of adoration does not primarily aim at edifying, elevating, purifying or consecrating the worshipers. To be sure, it should bring about all these results, but they are only its by-products. The purpose of worship is to ascribe glory to God."[26]

---

[26]   Terrien, *Psalms and Their Meaning*, xi.

Our People, Our Places, Our Faith

The great 18th century revivalist John Wesley was the catalyst for an expansive revival within the Church of England. It quickly spread to young America where it came to be known as "Methodism." The societies Wesley established in order to disciple the tens of thousands of newly awakened churchgoers and converts would eventually shape the "Wesleyan" evangelical movement throughout the world. Being an apostle of sorts to these new communities of faith, Wesley thought it important to offer direction for congregational worship. As a result, he published a tract known as "Directions for Singing," which may be found in the front of the United Methodist Hymnal. And so, in an age of reserve and restraint, Wesley taught his disciples seven points regarding singing, including the following:

1. Sing all: See that you join with the congregation as frequently as you can. Let not a slight degree of weakness or weariness hinder you. If it is a cross to you, take it up and you will find a blessing.
2. Sing lustily and with a good courage. Beware of singing as if you were half dead, or half asleep; but lift up your voice with strength. Be no more afraid of your voice now, nor more ashamed of its being heard, than when you sung the songs of Satan.
3. Above all sing spiritually. Have an eye to God in every word you sing. Aim at pleasing him more than yourself, or any other creature. In order to do this, attend strictly to the sense of what you sing, and see that your heart is not carried away with the sound, but offered to God continually; so shall your singing be such as the Lord will approve of here, and reward you when he comes in the clouds of heaven.[27]

These instructions make me chuckle a bit, but they also convict me. "Beware of singing as if you were half dead," says the preacher. Bring it, John Wesley!

---

[27] Wesley, "Directions for Singing," vii.

Day 3: The Power

First Contact

When we gutted our hundred-year-old house in Wheaton, Illinois, it was a story of jackhammers, whirling plaster, and plumbing and wiring that hadn't seen the light of day since World War II. When the contractors *finally* went home, it was time to choose a color scheme. This should be the fun part, right? Wrong. I had never started from scratch before and I was overwhelmed. So, I had a heart-to-heart with an interior decorator friend and I learned something that completely blew my mind. Did you know that there is a FORMULA for color-scheming your house?! A formula that *always* works and makes you look like Martha Stewart? You want to know what it is, don't you? Well, because I love you, I am going to share the secret: 60-30-10. That's it, those are the magic numbers. Throughout your entire house choose three colors. Just three. And repeat them in every room in one of these percentages. Your decorating life will never be the same. Why does this work? Because the human brain, and eye, and ear love repetition.

Into the Book

As we will discuss in our video lesson, the power of poetry and the power of song should not be taken lightly. What we commit to music, we memorize. What we memorize, shapes us. As Mark Noll says, "what evangelicals have been is what we have sung."[28] So, it is important that our worship songs embody and communicate sound theology.

It is also important that our sung worship be beautiful. Because what the ear and mind love, the ear and mind remember. Let's take a look at Psalm 91 and ask ourselves how this song is *true* and how this song is *beautiful*. How would this psalm, set to music, shape us?

Turn back to this lesson's Real Time and Space and review what you learn there about Hebrew poetry. Recall that *repetition* is the stuff of Hebrew poetry. The repetition can come in diads or triads, synonymous

---

28   Noll, "We Are What We Sing," 37.

or antithetical thoughts, chiastic or ring compositions. As you read through Psalm 91 look for different types of repetition, highlighting or somehow indicating (box, circle, underline, etc.) the repeated elements.

○ A and as a matter of fact B: (see for example v. 1)

○ A and even more so B: (see for example v. 3)

○ See if you can find an example of a chiastic structure. Recall this structure follows this pattern: A B B A. (Hint: it is near the end of the psalm!)

Psalm 91

[1] Whoever dwells in the shelter of the Most
    High
    will rest in the shadow of the
    Almighty.
[2] I will say of the LORD, "He is my refuge and
    my fortress,
    my God, in whom I trust."

[3] Surely he will save you
    from the fowler's snare
    and from the deadly pestilence.
[4] He will cover you with his feathers,
    and under his wings you will find refuge;
    his faithfulness will be your shield and
    rampart.
[5] You will not fear the terror of night,
    nor the arrow that flies by day,
[6] nor the pestilence that stalks in the darkness,
    nor the plague that destroys at midday.

[7] A thousand may fall at your side,
    ten thousand at your right hand,
    but it will not come near you.
[8] You will only observe with your eyes
    and see the punishment of the wicked.

[9] If you say, "The LORD is my refuge,"
    and you make the Most High your dwelling,
[10] no harm will overtake you,
    no disaster will come near your tent.
[11] For he will command his angels concerning
    you
    to guard you in all your ways;
[12] they will lift you up in their hands,
    so that you will not strike your foot against
    a stone.
[13] You will tread on the lion and the cobra;
    you will trample the great lion and
    the serpent.

[14] "Because he loves me," says the LORD, "I will
  rescue him;
  I will protect him, for he acknowledges my
  name.
[15] He will call on me, and I will answer him;

I will be with him in trouble,
  I will deliver him and honor him.
[16] With long life I will satisfy him
  and show him my salvation."

Real People, Real Places, Real Faith

Our psalm is identified by Franz Delitzsch as a "Talismanic Song in Time of War and Pestilence."[29] He divides the piece into several voices. The first voice is that of the liturgist who assures the congregation of the power and faithfulness of their God (vv. 1, 3–8). The second voice is that of the congregation, claiming for their own the words of the liturgist, "[Yahweh] is my refuge and my fortress!" (vv. 2, 9). The third voice is that of God himself, who, once the liturgist has declared God's seemingly impossible intentions for those who love him, adds his reassurance to those already spoken: "Because he loves me, I will rescue him; I will protect him, for he acknowledges my name!" (vv. 14). The promises offered to the believer rise higher and higher throughout the piece: "He will command his angels concerning you to guard you in all your ways; they will lift you up in their hands, so that you will not strike your foot against a stone" (vv. 11–12; see also Mark 16:18; Luke 10:19). And as the song progresses, so too the use of metaphor and personification. God is a fortified tower; he is an adult eagle on the cliffs defending his young; he is the hunter who turns his captive loose. Danger that comes at night or high noon is intercepted in this hymn. Even the lion and the deadly cobra will do the worshiper no harm. As we engage this psalm, we need to realize that all the dangers named in it are real ones in Israel's world. But they are also all the most extreme of dangers. Can you picture the average Israelite gathered for worship being led through this song? Can you imagine the power of a worship service when the community of faith gathers to remind each other who their God is and who they are, and the power of Heaven comes cascading down?

---

[29] Delitzsch, *Commentary on the Old Testament*, 60–62.

Our People, Our Places, Our Faith

I am writing this guide in the midst of the Covid-19 pandemic. Right now, December 2020, the numbers are frightening—more infections and deaths than at any point since the virus began its deadly journey across the globe. Tens of thousands are praying for protection. And the answers offered to the faithful of David's day are offered to us as well: "You will not fear the terror of the night, nor the arrow that flies by day, nor the pestilence that stalks in the darkness, nor the plague that destroys at midday (Ps 91:5–6)." Psalm 91 is the perfect psalm for this dark hour. The danger is real. A thousand have fallen at your side, ten thousand at your right hand (v. 7). But the very fact that you are reading this guide means that the Lord of the Cosmos has chosen to spare you. For what purpose? We will see. But whatever comes your way, know that the words of this ancient hymn are as true today as they were then: "He who dwells in the shelter of the Most High will rest in the shadow of the Almighty" (v. 1).

Day 4: A Psalm

First Contact

Mark Noll tells us that "[d]iligent preaching, an incredible organizational energy and learned theology have gone into the creation of modern evangelicalism. But nothing so profoundly defined the faith of evangelicalism as its hymnody: what evangelicals have been is what we have sung."[30] Our song shapes our faith. Our faith shapes our song. As you ponder Psalm 71, how might this ancient testimony of faith shape your faith today?

Read through Psalm 71 on the following page once (preferably out loud) without stopping to take notes. Then follow the instructions in Reading & Observing in your second reading.

---

[30] Noll, "We Are What We Sing," 37.

Psalm 71

[1] In you, LORD, I have taken refuge;
    let me never be put to shame.
[2] In your righteousness, rescue me and deliver
    me;
    turn your ear to me and save me.
[3] Be my rock of refuge,
    to which I can always go;
give the command to save me,
    for you are my rock and my fortress.
[4] Deliver me, my God, from the hand of the
    wicked,
    from the grasp of those who are evil and
    cruel.

[5] For you have been my hope, Sovereign LORD,
    my confidence since my youth.
[6] From birth I have relied on you;
    you brought me forth from my
    mother's womb.
    I will ever praise you.
[7] I have become a sign to many;
    you are my strong refuge.
[8] My mouth is filled with your praise,
    declaring your splendor all day long.

[9] Do not cast me away when I am old;
    do not forsake me when my strength is
    gone.

[10] For my enemies speak against me;
    those who wait to kill me conspire together.
[11] They say, "God has forsaken him;
    pursue him and seize him,
    for no one will rescue him."
[12] Do not be far from me, my God;
    come quickly, God, to help me.
[13] May my accusers perish in shame;
    may those who want to harm me
    be covered with scorn and disgrace.

[14] As for me, I will always have hope;
    I will praise you more and more.

[15] My mouth will tell of your righteous deeds,
    of your saving acts all day long—
    though I know not how to relate them all.
[16] I will come and proclaim your mighty acts,
    Sovereign LORD;
    I will proclaim your righteous deeds, yours
    alone.
[17] Since my youth, God, you have taught me,
    and to this day I declare your marvelous
    deeds.
[18] Even when I am old and gray,
    do not forsake me, my God,
    till I declare your power to the next
    generation,
    your mighty acts to all who are to come.

19 Your righteousness, God, reaches to
    the heavens,
    you who have done great things.
    Who is like you, God?
20 Though you have made me see troubles,
    many and bitter,
    you will restore my life again;
from the depths of the earth
    you will again bring me up.
21 You will increase my honor
    and comfort me once more.

22 I will praise you with the harp
    for your faithfulness, my God;
I will sing praise to you with the lyre,
    Holy One of Israel.
23 My lips will shout for joy
    when I sing praise to you—
    I whom you have delivered.
24 My tongue will tell of your righteous acts
    all day long,
for those who wanted to harm me
    have been put to shame and confusion.

Reading & Observing

Read through the psalm again, this time looking for these things:

○ Which collection does the psalm belong to (Book I, II, III, IV, V)?

○ Is there a superscript? If so, what is it? Who is the psalm attributed to?

○ What type of psalm is it? (What is the psalmist doing: praying, praising, complaining, giving thanks, etc.?)

○ Whom does the psalmist declare God to be to him? Circle these words.

○ Choose a color pen or pencil to highlight the requests/petitions the psalmist makes to God for himself.

○ Choose another color to highlight the psalmist's requests to God against his enemies.

○ Where does he appeal to God's care in the past?

○ Place boxes around the psalmist's vows to God.

Responding

Jack Salberg is my colleague. He is a world-class biologist, but more importantly to him, Jack is a dad. And one day Jack got the call that makes every parent tremble. There had been an accident. His son was lying in the wreckage of a flipped car on the side of an embankment—with a ruptured aorta. The doctors told Jack that 90% of those with such an injury never make it to the hospital. Of those that do, 90% don't come home. Jack's son survived. Jack's son came home. But the doctors warned the family that it isn't at all uncommon for adolescents who've had such a near death experience to regress during their recovery. Jack's son did. And so Jack camped out on the living room floor for weeks. When his son was finally ready to move back to his bed, for a full year Jack read Narnia or played guitar to him. Then there were the years of lingering neurological issues—different sides of his body had different temperatures; periodically his son would wake up and find he couldn't walk. The specialists were unsure whether he'd ever come back.

Then one day Jack walked into the house and found his son with his Bible open, reading Psalm 71. His son looked up at him with tears in his eyes and the words came tumbling out: "Dad, I'm not sure the Bible has ever spoken to me like this before. But 'As for me, I will always have hope; I will praise you more and more' (Ps 71:14). Dad, I want to fight and I'd like to have this tattooed on me." Jack demurred, "We have the Bible written on our hearts son, we don't need it written on our bodies." "I know, Dad, but I want to write it on my body, for when my heart forgets." Just reading these words brings tears to my eyes . . . "for when my heart forgets." The gift of the book of Psalms is that it prays for us when we can't, it reminds us of our inheritance "when our heart forgets." And so Jack's son got his tattoo—line one of Psalm 71:14. And a few years later, when this young man successfully hiked the entire Muir Trail—he added the second line to his tattoo. What did Athanasius say? "The Psalms have a unique place in the Bible . . . [whereas] most of Scripture speaks *to* us, the Psalms speak *for* us." Are you in a space where you can't find the words or the energy to pray for yourself? Let the ancients pray for you.

○ Sing the psalm! Go to **http://psalms.seedbed.com/** and navigate your way to Psalm 71. Choose one (or all!) of the tune options there and sing this psalm to the Lord.

○ Illustrate the psalm! There are pages set aside at the back of the book (pages 209–217) for you to create your own illuminated psalms as well as a sample to get your creative juices flowing.

○ Pray the psalm! Put in your own names and places, and let the ancients pray with you!

○ Choose one paragraph of this psalm to memorize.

○ Set this psalm to your own music. Let the words find their way into your heart.

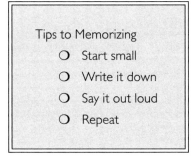

Tips to Memorizing
○ Start small
○ Write it down
○ Say it out loud
○ Repeat

SESSION 5

The Power
of Poetry

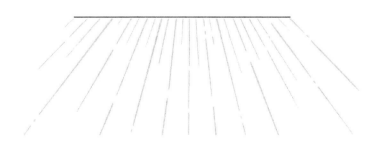

SESSION 5: GROUP MEETING

Schedule

GROUP MEETING
Session 5 Video Teaching and Discussion

INDIVIDUAL STUDY
Day 1: The Sheep
Day 2: The Shepherd
Day 3: The Ultimate Shepherd
Day 4: A Psalm

Debrief & Discover

Ask your group members to name at least three characteristics of poetry that distinguishes it from prose.

Have each person share one of their favorite poems or poets/songs or songwriters and why it is their favorite.

Watch Session 5 Video:
THE POWER OF POETRY
(19 minutes)

Video Notes

These are provided for you and your group members to follow along during the video as well as to offer room for note taking (writing down questions and aha moments as you like).

    I.   **What is poetry?**

        A. **Elevated speech, high eloquence designed to move and to persuade**

        B. **Depends on a rhythmic structure using meter or rhyme**

        C. **Tends toward metrical scheme and often some element of rhyme**

        D. **Some examples**

II. What is it about poetry and music that gets into our souls?

   A. Congregations singing together, reciting creeds together

   B. Andrew Peterson's "Is He Worthy?"

   C. Tell the Story and tell it well

III. What is Hebrew poetic style?

   A. The "seconding sentence"

   B. A rhythm of sense

   C. Repetition

   D. Examples

      1. Psalm 1

      2. Psalm 100

      3. See also Luke 1:46–55 (Mary's Song)

Dialogue, Digest & Do

❍ What *is* it about poetry, about music, about art that gets into our souls in a way that prose cannot?

❍ What is it about a congregation singing out their declaration of faith together or reciting their creed together that transforms the words into something almost metaphysical, something that unifies and defines, that emboldens and strengthens?

❍ Why it is necessary to sing together or recite our creeds *together* in our congregations?

In answering the question about why it is necessary to sing together and recite our creeds together, Sandy says we need to tell the Story and to tell it well. We need to whisper it in the darkness; we need to shout it in the shadows. We need to write it in our hearts, recite it in the morning and at night until we believe it and can live it, until we can see beyond the darkness of the day.

Challenge your group members to commit to writing at least one entire psalm on their hearts by memorizing it by the end of our eight weeks together. Perhaps as a group you can choose a psalm to memorize together, or you could have your members choose a partner to work with to hold each other accountable.

Next Week

Next week we'll be diving into perhaps the most often quoted psalm of all time . . . any guesses as to which one that is?

Closing Prayer

Ask your group members if there is anything they would like prayer for—especially something highlighted by this week's video. How's that list coming?

Reminder: If you are behind in the reading, pick up with the individual study tomorrow to get back on track.

SESSION 5: INDIVIDUAL STUDY

Lord, Like a Shepherd Lead Us

A Word from Sandy

In the beautiful verse of the King James Version, Psalm 95:6–7 declares, "O come, let us worship and bow down: let us kneel before the LORD our maker. For he is our God; and we are the people of his pasture, and the sheep of his hand." I know very well that "sheep of his hand" communicates the "sheep under his authority," or even the "livestock over whom he has direction." But somehow this practical and transparent language of responsible animal husbandry does not spark in me the same response as the lyric verse, "the sheep of his hand." And I'm guessing it is the same for you. We are indeed "the sheep of his hand"—the creatures for whom he has chosen to accept responsibility, the helpless flock that he has sworn to protect, the hapless ones who need his daily direction. And how grateful I am that he has obligated himself to such a menial role for a hapless creature such as I.

Our text this week is probably the most well-known Psalm of your Old Testament, Psalm 23. I sometimes speak of it as "a psalm for sheep and shepherds" because this psalm speaks as directly to the sheep (congregation) as it does to the shepherds (pastors). This psalm comes from the very first collection within the Psalter. It is a psalm of David (the shepherd). It is a hymn of praise, and it rests upon our hearts the way a cup of good coffee or chamomile tea rests within our chilled hands on a crisp, bright November morning.

My ambition in our lessons this week is to make what is old new, what is familiar unfamiliar, and to thereby remind you and me who we are, *whose* we are, and encourage you with the inalterable truth of your inheritance. We are *indeed* the "sheep of his hand." Let's get started, shall we?

Real Time & Space

Did you know that the book of Psalms is quoted more frequently in the New Testament than any other book of the Old Testament? Did you know that there are more fragments of the book of Psalms among the Dead Sea

Scrolls than any other book of Scripture, and that Judaism has evolved with an exceptionally high value placed on the book as well? Why might that be? Well, New Testament scholar Ronald Cox states: "I am inclined to think that their preservation [the psalms] and their being so highly regarded is indebted to the attribution of the Psalms to David. Davidic authorship tied to the hope of the restoration of the kingdom of Israel make the Psalms visionary texts about a reconstituted relationship with God and the world. . . . David's authorship becomes the basis for reading the psalms as prophecy."[31]

So, what is it about Davidic authorship that appeals to both Old and New Testament authors? I would argue it is what rhetoric would call "ethos"—the credibility of the speaker. Rhetoric teaches us that when *logos* (logical and credible content), *pathos* (engagement of higher passions), and *ethos* (the trustworthiness and integrity of the speaker) come together in a presentation, the audience is compelled to respond. David's ethos is that he was the paradigmatic king of all Israel. All the kings of Israel are compared to David for good or for ill before the account of the monarchy is complete, and the last four verses of the national history in 2 Kings are wholly focused on the fate of his one remaining legitimate heir. It was David's steadfast allegiance to the God of Israel that won him that status—even though he was also known for seriously blowing it on more than one occasion. I like to review David's life in light of Proverbs 24:16: "The righteous man falls seven times; and gets up eight" (Richter's translation).

Over and over again in the annals of 1 and 2 Samuel we are introduced to a man who is in no way perfect but is in every way loyal. Where are his loyalties? Whose kingdom is he building? To whom does he bow the knee when disciplined? Yahweh. Always Yahweh. Only Yahweh. It is this kind of integrity that inspired the LORD's word to the prophet Samuel regarding Jesse's youngest son: "The LORD does not look at the things people look at. People look at the outward appearance, but the LORD looks at the heart" (1 Sam 16:7).

David's humble roots, his identity as an "unlikely leader," and his willingness to stand up for his God and his people despite impossible odds inspired others to believe that they too could overcome their circumstances with character and courage. As a result, 1 and 2 Samuel are all about David and how his integrity triumphed over disadvantage, corruption, and bias time and time again. You can hardly turn a page of the national history (1 Sam–2 Kgs) without hearing some reference to "my servant David" and Yahweh's intent to bless Israel "because of my servant David."[32] So this guy's got chops. And when David speaks about devotion and submission and hope and suffering . . . people listen.

---

[31] Cox, "The New Testament Preaches the Psalms," 86. See for example Hebrews 3:6–4:11.
[32] See for instance 2 Sam 3:18; 7:5, 8; 1 Kgs 11:36, 38; 14:8 for "my servant David" or "David my servant." For examples of "for the sake of David my servant" or "for the sake of my servant David" see 1 Kgs 11:13, 32, 34; 2 Kgs 19:34; 20:6 (NIV).

Day 1: The Sheep

First Contact

Phillip Keller grew up in East Africa surrounded by herders. He also spent eight years as a sheep owner and sheep rancher garnering "firsthand experience with every phase of sheep management."[33] In his devotional titled *A Shepherd Looks at the 23rd Psalm*, Keller has this to say: "It is no accident that God has chosen to call us sheep. The behaviour of sheep and human beings is similar in many ways. . . . Our mass mind (mob instincts), our fears and timidity, our stubbornness and stupidity, our perverse habits are all parallels of profound importance."[34]

Into the Book

All of us know at least some of the words to Psalm 23, "The LORD is my shepherd." All of us know that Jesus claims to be "the good shepherd." In our video lesson this week we're going to learn why the image of a shepherd with his or her sheep is so dominant in our Bibles and so regularly frequents our faith lives. So let's prepare by diving in to the most famous "sheep" psalm of all, Psalm 23. A psalm of David.

Psalm 23:1

"The LORD is my shepherd"

○ If Yahweh is David's shepherd, what does that make David?

We'll look more at David as a shepherd in tomorrow's lesson. For now, read 1 Samuel 17:34–37 with an eye toward what we learn about sheep.

---

[33] Keller, *Shepherd Trilogy*, 6.
[34] Keller, *Shepherd Trilogy*, 14.

I Samuel 17:34-37

[34] But David said to Saul, "Your servant has been keeping his father's sheep. When a lion or a bear came and carried off a sheep from the flock, [35] I went after it, struck it and rescued the sheep from its mouth. When it turned on me, I seized it by its hair, struck it and killed it. [36] Your servant has killed both the lion and the bear; this uncircumcised Philistine will be like one of them, because he has defied the armies of the living God. [37] The Lord who rescued me from the paw of the lion and the paw of the bear will rescue me from the hand of this Philistine."

❍ Based on this passage, what is something that sheep need?

Psalm 23:2–3

[2] He makes me lie down in green pastures,
　　he leads me beside quiet waters,
[3] he refreshes my soul.
He guides me along the right paths
　　for his name's sake.

❍ Based on this passage, what do you think sheep need?

❍ Do a Google search on "Awassi Sheep" (the breed raised in Israel in David's day) and find out three things about "sheep needs" that you didn't know before. Then pool your information with your group members . . . and maybe have a little sheep competition!

Let's look at a few more. Underline the phrase that is repeated in all three of these passages. What does this phrase tell you about the people? About their God?

Psalm 74:1

O God, why have you rejected us forever?
Why does your anger smolder against the sheep of your pasture?

Psalm 79:13

Then we your people, the sheep of your pasture,

> will praise you forever;

from generation to generation

> we will proclaim your praise.

Psalm 100:1–3

¹ Shout for joy to the LORD, all the earth.

> ² Worship the Lord with gladness;

> come before him with joyful songs

³ Know that the Lord is God.

> It is he who made us, and we are his;

> we are his people, the sheep of his pasture.

Real People, Real Places, Real Faith

Why is there so much talk about sheep and shepherds in our Bibles? Why do the words *sheep, goat, lamb, flock, cattle, herd, pasture,* and *staff* show up in so many contexts? The answer is kind of obvious—our heroes were pastoralists. Abraham, Isaac, Jacob and his sons, Moses, and David all kept sheep. This was their occupation, these were the "metaphors they lived by," and these folks understood the way of sheep.

So let's talk about sheep. The most common livestock to be found on an Israelite homestead were mixed flocks of Black Sinai goats and Awassi ("fat-tailed") sheep. As we'll discuss in the video, the "mixed" element involved the fact that these two animals cohabit very well, and the additional reality that having a 60/40 split ensured economic stability. Both animals were kept for their milk and meat, but the Awassi sheep was by far the more valuable animal. This was partly because their meat was preferred over goat and partly because they produced more milk, but it was primarily because of their renowned fleece. If life went smoothly, Awassi sheep brought their owners significant economic returns—the "stocks" of an ancient investment portfolio. The Black Sinai goat was not as valuable. A reliable provider of milk and meat, yes, but its coarse hair was utilized only for tent curtains, bags, and other "rough" textiles.

So why keep goats at all? Well, although the Awassi sheep were the more productive investment, they were also the more vulnerable asset. As Timothy Laniak details, Awassi sheep are terribly nearsighted, get lost easily, and also panic easily.[35] So when one of these sheep gets lost (as they are wont to do), they typically hunker down and begin to cry—a very effective way to locate the nearest predator. Black Sinai goats, on the other hand, are tough as nails. They have been indigenous to the region for centuries, are obnoxiously individual, and very capable of returning to an undomesticated state if needed. The Sinai goat has an extremely high tolerance for heat and drought. They will eat just about anything, and even during the hottest part of the season only need to be watered once every four days. Goats were therefore the "bonds" of the Israelite farmer's portfolio. Even if the market went south, the goats didn't.[36]

Our People, Our Places, Our Faith

Let's ponder this idea that God compares us to sheep. As is so typical of our God, he has chosen a metaphor that his people understood. *Everyone* in the world of the Bible had some sort of hands-on experience with sheep and shepherds. David, who is credited with this psalm, knew *a lot* about sheep. Now that we know something about the metaphor, let's pause over what it means to have the Lord as our shepherd and to be "the sheep of his hand." Essentially, God is announcing that he has taken responsibility for us. That it is his job to defend us against the lion and the bear because we are an essential part of his household. As with Said, who you'll meet in the next session, God is affirming that the life of the flock is just as important as the life of the shepherd. Within the embrace of this chosen metaphor, God is claiming us in our smelly stupidity and stepping in to lead, protect, and nurture our nearsighted selves. He is taking his position as our guide and defender and putting his life in the balance for ours. Why? Because God knows, we are "prone to wander," and his ambition is "to seek and to save what was lost."[37]

35 Laniak, *Shepherds After My Own Heart*, 42–57.
36 Richter, *Stewards of Eden*, 31–32.
37 Luke 19:10; Robert Robinson, "Come Thou Fount of Every Blessing," 1758.

Day 2: The Shepherd

First Contact

George Adam Smith (1856–1942) was a Scottish theologian and one of the earliest historical geographers of Palestine. In his early 19th century horseback study tour of the territory, he was mesmerized by the shepherds he encountered in this ancient land: "On some high moor, across which at night hyenas howl, when you meet him, sleepless, far-sighted, weather beaten, armed, leaning on his staff, and looking out over his scattered sheep, every one on his heart, you understand why the shepherd of Judea sprang to the front in his people's history; why they gave his name to their king, and made him the symbol of Providence; why Christ took him as the type of self-sacrifice."[38]

Into the Book

In the last lesson, we looked at sheep. We learned that sheep cannot protect themselves, they are not smart, and they can be fragile. We learned that sheep need a shepherd. Today we look at shepherds. We'll begin with David.

Read 1 Samuel 17:14–15, 28, 34–37 and Psalm 78:70–72.

> [14] David was the youngest. The three oldest followed Saul [into battle against the Philistines], [15] but David went back and forth from Saul to tend his father's sheep at Bethlehem.
>
> [28] When Eliab, David's oldest brother, heard him [David] speaking with the men, he burned with anger at him and asked, "Why have you come down here? And with whom did you leave those few sheep in the wilderness? I know how conceited you are and how wicked your heart is; you came down only to watch the battle."

---

[38]   Smith, *Historical Geography of the Holy Land*, 311–12.

Now take a look at David's words to Saul in 1 Samuel 17. The Philistine army had come ready to fight the Israelite army. But when Saul and the Israelites saw Goliath, a giant decked out in armor the Israelite men had never seen before, they were "dismayed and terrified" (v. 11). Rather than stepping up to fight, our guys turned tail and fled (v. 24). Taking food to his brothers who are with the Israelite army, David hears Goliath's words, is appalled, and says (v. 26): "Who is this uncircumcised Philistine that he should defy the armies of the living God?" When David eagerly volunteers to face the giant, King Saul basically tells him, "Sorry, kid, you're too young."

We read David's response to Saul in yesterday's study found in 1 Samuel 17:34–37. Turn back there and reread the passage now with an eye toward David as a shepherd.

○ What does David know about shepherding?

○ Based on these passages, write out a job description for a good shepherd.

○ Do you think David is a good shepherd or a bad shepherd?

Good shepherds take care of their flocks; they are willing to sacrifice themselves for the safety of the sheep, that's what they do. So, what do you think *bad* shepherds do? The passage we're looking at comes from Ezekiel 34. Ezekiel is of course speaking about the exile.

If you refer to the timeline graphic on page 130–131, you will see that what Ezekiel is speaking of as "the scattering" is the exile in 586 BCE. The great watershed of Israelite history. That horrific moment when the curses of the covenant at Mount Sinai come home to roost. The people of Israel are stripped of their land, their homes, their flocks, their children, even their lives. Because of the unending, uncorrected rebellion of Israel, God finally says "enough." The armies of the Babylonian empire flood over the land promised to Abraham, and his descendants are dragged off as slaves of another kingdom.[39] And all of this heart-wrenching loss is blamed on the shepherds. You did not keep my flock. You thought it was yours. You were wrong.

Ezekiel 34:1–16

[1] The word of the Lord came to me: [2] "Son of man, prophesy against the shepherds of Israel; prophesy and say to them: 'This is what the Sovereign Lord says: Woe to you shepherds of Israel who only take care of yourselves! Should not shepherds take care of the flock? [3] You eat the curds, clothe yourselves with the wool and slaughter the choice animals, but you do not take care of the flock. [4] You have not strengthened the weak or healed the sick or bound up the injured. You have not brought back the strays or searched for the lost. You have ruled them harshly and brutally. [5] So they were scattered because there was no shepherd, and when they were scattered they became food for all the wild animals. [6] My sheep wandered over all the mountains and on every high hill. They were scattered over the whole earth, and no one searched or looked for them.

[7] "'Therefore, you shepherds, hear the word of the Lord: [8] As surely as I live, declares the Sovereign Lord, because my flock lacks a shepherd and so has been plundered and has become food for all the wild animals, and because my shepherds did not search for my flock but cared for themselves rather than for my flock, [9] therefore, you shepherds, hear the word of the Lord: [10] This is what the Sovereign Lord says: I am against the shepherds and will hold them accountable for my flock. I will remove them from tending the flock so that the shepherds can no longer feed themselves. I will rescue my flock from their mouths, and it will no longer be food for them.

[11] "'For this is what the Sovereign Lord says: I myself will search for my sheep and look after them. [12] As a shepherd looks after his scattered flock when he is with them, so will I look after my sheep. I will rescue them from all the places where they were scattered on a day of clouds and

---

[39] See 2 Kings 17:7–23; 24:1–4.

darkness. [13] I will bring them out from the nations and gather them from the countries, and I will bring them into their own land. I will pasture them on the mountains of Israel, in the ravines and in all the settlements in the land. [14] I will tend them in a good pasture, and the mountain heights of Israel will be their grazing land. There they will lie down in good grazing land, and there they will feed in a rich pasture on the mountains of Israel. [15] I myself will tend my sheep and have them lie down, declares the Sovereign Lord. [16] I will search for the lost and bring back the strays. I will bind up the injured and strengthen the weak, but the sleek and the strong I will destroy. I will shepherd the flock with justice.'"

○ To whom is Ezekiel speaking? Who are they?

○ Choose two colors of pens or colored pencils. Use one color to highlight what the shepherds were doing. Use the other color to highlight what they were not doing.

○ What was the result?

○ Choose one more color and highlight everything that Yahweh says he will do.

PATRIARCHAL

Eden
??

Noah
??

Abraham/Isaac/Jacob
c. 2000 BCE [c.1850 BCE]

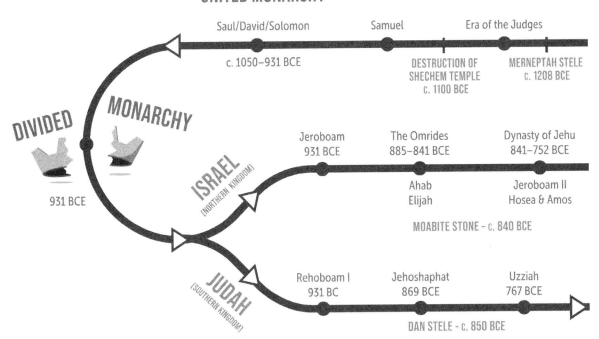

UNITED MONARCHY

Saul/David/Solomon
c. 1050–931 BCE

Samuel

Era of the Judges

DESTRUCTION OF
SHECHEM TEMPLE
c. 1100 BCE

MERNEPTAH STELE
c. 1208 BCE

DIVIDED MONARCHY
931 BCE

ISRAEL
(NORTHERN KINGDOM)

Jeroboam
931 BCE

The Omrides
885–841 BCE

Dynasty of Jehu
841–752 BCE

Ahab
Elijah

Jeroboam II
Hosea & Amos

MOABITE STONE – c. 840 BCE

JUDAH
(SOUTHERN KINGDOM)

Rehoboam I
931 BC

Jehoshaphat
869 BCE

Uzziah
767 BCE

DAN STELE – c. 850 BCE

2ND TEMPLE JUDAISM

Hasmoneans
152–64 BCE

Alexander
336 BCE

Ezra & Nehemiah
458–433 BCE

Malachi

Rebuilding the Temple
520–515 BCE

Haggai & Zechariah

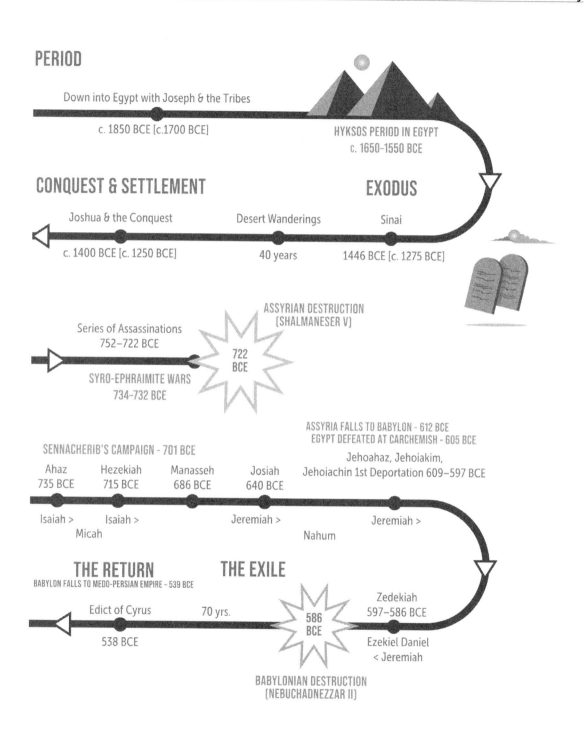

PERIOD

Down into Egypt with Joseph & the Tribes

c. 1850 BCE [c.1700 BCE]

HYKSOS PERIOD IN EGYPT
c. 1650-1550 BCE

CONQUEST & SETTLEMENT

Joshua & the Conquest

c. 1400 BCE [c. 1250 BCE]

Desert Wanderings

40 years

EXODUS

Sinai

1446 BCE [c. 1275 BCE]

ASSYRIAN DESTRUCTION
(SHALMANESER V)

Series of Assassinations
752–722 BCE

722
BCE

SYRO-EPHRAIMITE WARS
734-732 BCE

ASSYRIA FALLS TO BABYLON - 612 BCE
EGYPT DEFEATED AT CARCHEMISH - 605 BCE

SENNACHERIB'S CAMPAIGN - 701 BCE

Jehoahaz, Jehoiakim,
Jehoiachin 1st Deportation 609–597 BCE

Ahaz	Hezekiah	Manasseh	Josiah
735 BCE	715 BCE	686 BCE	640 BCE

Isaiah >   Isaiah >   Jeremiah >   Jeremiah >

Micah   Nahum

THE RETURN

BABYLON FALLS TO MEDO-PERSIAN EMPIRE – 539 BCE

THE EXILE

Zedekiah
597–586 BCE

Edict of Cyrus   70 yrs.

586
BCE

538 BCE

Ezekiel Daniel
< Jeremiah

BABYLONIAN DESTRUCTION
(NEBUCHADNEZZAR II)

Real People, Real Places, Real Faith

Just as the wilderness is the natural environment for flocks, so too is it the natural environment for wolves. Jeremiah speaks of "a wolf from the desert" (5:1), what the wildlife experts would identify as the "Arabian wolf" of the biblical world. Small for a wolf, weighing in at about 45 pounds, its size has helped it adapt to life in a desert climate. Although opportunistic eaters, the wolves of the Negev can take down any domestic animal up to the size of an adult goat—lambs and kids were ideal prey. Thus, wolves have been the enemy of the shepherd for millennia. As we move through the biblical text, we see that for David "wolves" were actually wolves. For Ezekiel, they were the predatorial religions of Canaan that seduced Israel to "follow after other gods" (hear the flock language?), and foreign oppressors who "devoured" the people of God. For Jesus and Paul, the "wolves" were false teachers whose ambition was to use the flock for their own ends (Matt 7:15; 10:16). In Acts 20:27–31, Paul instructs the Ephesian elders to therefore "be on your guard," ready to defend the flock from false teachers who seek to "draw away" members of the community in the same fashion that a wolf would seek to isolate a ewe with her lamb. These images harken back to George Adam Smith's description of the good shepherds—they are armed.

Our People, Our Places, Our Faith

As you will hear in our video lesson, Israel didn't *create* the idea of shepherd as leader; they inherited it. This because everyone in Israel's world knew what a good shepherd looked like, and what a bad shepherd looked like. And no one wanted their flock kept by a bad shepherd. Similar to Bill Gates's "10 Rules for Success," good shepherds work hard, they take risks, they endure discomfort, they love what they do. Moreover, the leadership gurus also often comment that although many people think that good leadership means being popular most of the time, in reality, good leadership means the leader needs to be willing to be highly unpopular with some people for part of the time. Jesus said it this way: "Woe to you when everyone speaks well of you, for that is how their ancestors treated the false prophets" (Luke 6:26). And, of course, the "false prophets" are the wolves of the New Testament.

As we think about our current contexts, can I say that it is always incredibly difficult to call out false teaching and false teachers. Especially if those teachers are among your own community. But our Good Shepherd, Jesus, and his first-century under-shepherds make it clear that it must be done. Good leaders defend their people. Good pastors do not "shrink away" from conflict; they defend the flock. Our great Shepherd was persecuted, slandered, marginalized, and eventually executed for speaking the truth and standing up to corruption. If we choose to take up the staff of leadership, should we expect anything different?

Day 3: The Ultimate Shepherd

First Contact

There is one more group of sheep and shepherds that need our attention before we leave this lesson. This group is rarely associated with Psalm 23 or with kings and crowns and symbols of leadership. These are the shepherds who Luke is at pains to tell us about in his Gospel—the very first to hear the "good news" and to respond in faith. These are our sleepless heroes of Bethlehem, greeted by a huge and scary angel, who appeared at the Nativity looking for the King of kings. These were indeed good shepherds, as the text tells us they were sleeping outside in order to protect their flocks (2:8), but they are typically presented as impoverished, common laborers. The wealth of Abraham, Jacob, and Jesse has no place in this story. Yet these shepherds are the first to greet the king. The king who they found in a stable, lying in a manger. How appropriate, how lovely, that the first to recognize the arrival of the Chief Shepherd, were shepherds themselves.

Into the Book

We begin today with a look at Micah the prophet and what he has to say about the one who will come and then look at how Matthew uses this prophecy in relating the story of Jesus's birth.

Micah 5:2, 4

2 "But you, Bethlehem Ephrathah,
   though you are small among the clans of Judah,
out of you will come for me
   one who will be ruler over Israel,
whose origins are from of old,
   from ancient times."
4 He will stand and shepherd his flock
   in the strength of the Lord,
   in the majesty of the name of the Lord his God.
And they will live securely, for then his greatness
   will reach to the ends of the earth.

○ Speaking through Micah the prophet, who does Yahweh say will come? How does he describe him?

○ What will the one about whom Micah prophesies do?

Matthew 2:1–6

After Jesus was born in Bethlehem in Judea, during the time of King Herod, Magi from the east came to Jerusalem ² and asked, "Where is the one who has been born king of the Jews? We saw his star when it rose and have come to worship him."

³ When King Herod heard this he was disturbed, and all Jerusalem with him. ⁴ When he had called together all the people's chief priests and teachers of the law, he asked them where the Messiah was to be born. ⁵ "In Bethlehem in Judea," they replied, "for this is what the prophet has written:

⁶ "'But you, Bethlehem, in the land of Judah,
   are by no means least among the rulers of Judah;
for out of you will come a ruler
   who will shepherd my people Israel.'"

○ How does the author of Matthew use the prophecy from Micah?

Now read John to hear what Jesus has to say about sheep and about himself.

John 10:1–18

¹ "Very truly I tell you Pharisees, anyone who does not enter the sheep pen by the gate, but climbs in by some other way, is a thief and a robber. ² The one who enters by the gate is the shepherd of the sheep. ³ The gatekeeper opens the gate for him, and the sheep listen to his voice. He calls his own sheep by name and leads them out. ⁴ When he has brought out all his own, he goes on ahead of them, and his sheep follow him because they know his voice. ⁵ But they will never follow a stranger; in fact, they will run away from him because they do not recognize a stranger's voice." ⁶ Jesus used this figure of speech, but the Pharisees did not understand what he was telling them.

⁷ Therefore Jesus said again, "Very truly I tell you, I am the gate for the sheep. ⁸ All who have

come before me are thieves and robbers, but the sheep have not listened to them. [9] I am the gate; whoever enters through me will be saved. They will come in and go out, and find pasture. [10] The thief comes only to steal and kill and destroy; I have come that they may have life, and have it to the full.

[11] "I am the good shepherd. The good shepherd lays down his life for the sheep. [12] The hired hand is not the shepherd and does not own the sheep. So when he sees the wolf coming, he abandons the sheep and runs away. Then the wolf attacks the flock and scatters it. [13] The man runs away because he is a hired hand and cares nothing for the sheep.

[14] "I am the good shepherd; I know my sheep and my sheep know me—[15] just as the Father knows me and I know the Father—and I lay down my life for the sheep. [16] I have other sheep that are not of this sheep pen. I must bring them also. They too will listen to my voice, and there shall be one flock and one shepherd. [17] The reason my Father loves me is that I lay down my life—only to take it up again. [18] No one takes it from me, but I lay it down of my own accord. I have authority to lay it down and authority to take it up again. This command I received from my Father."

○ What do you learn about sheep in verses 1–6?

○ What do you know about sheep knowing the voice of their shepherd?

○ Highlight all of the places where Jesus says "I am . . . ." (for example, "I am the gate for the sheep").

○ Who are the sheep?

○ What does Jesus do for his sheep? Circle those things.

○ Who might a "stranger" be in the community of faith?

○ Who might a "wolf" be?

○ Who do you think the "other sheep" are?

Real People, Real Places, Real Faith

As we've moved through the studies this week, we've seen that Jesus corrects the many examples of failed leadership named in the prophet Ezekiel's critique of the kings of Israel with his own lived example. In that fashion, Jesus rehabilitates the image of shepherd and king for his people. Thus, in John 10:11 Jesus names himself the "good shepherd" who "lays down his life for the sheep." Like Said's father (as you will hear in the next video), Jesus announces that the life of the flock is just as important as the life of the shepherd. The good shepherd enters by the front gate (he doesn't sneak over the fence, John 10:1), he risks his life to defend the flock from predators (10:11–13), he calls his sheep by name . . . and they know him and they come (10:4, 14). In essence, Jesus is telling his disciples, "This is who I am. This is what I do. And this is what my under-shepherds are supposed to do as well."

Our People, Our Places, Our Faith

This brings us to **John 21:15–17**.

> [15] When they had finished eating, Jesus said to Simon Peter, "Simon son of John, do you love me more than these?"
>
> "Yes, Lord," he said, "you know that I love you."
>
> Jesus said, "Feed my lambs."
>
> [16] Again Jesus said, "Simon son of John, do you love me?"
>
> He answered, "Yes, Lord, you know that I love you."
>
> Jesus said, "Take care of my sheep."
>
> [17] The third time he said to him, "Simon son of John, do you love me?"
>
> Peter was hurt because Jesus asked him the third time, "Do you love me?" He said, "Lord, you know all things; you know that I love you."
>
> Jesus said, "Feed my sheep."

Tucked away in the first epistle that bears his name, the apostle Peter hearkens back to the lesson he learned on that chilly morning on the Sea of Galilee. Hear the words he, now the over-shepherd, has to say to his subordinates:

[1] To the elders among you, I appeal as a fellow elder and a witness of Christ's sufferings who also will share in the glory to be revealed: [2] Be shepherds of God's flock that is under your care, watching over them—not because you must, but because you are willing, as God wants you to be; not pursuing dishonest gain, but eager to serve; [3] not lording it over those entrusted to you, but being examples to the flock. [4] And when the Chief Shepherd appears, you will receive the crown of glory that will never fade away. (1 Pet 5:1–4)

Can you hear the echoes of that other conversation with the risen Christ back on the shores of the Sea of Galilee? Jesus was Peter's best friend and his mentor. Peter had sworn to protect him with his life. But when the wolves came . . . Peter ran. Instead of standing like a shepherd, Peter ran like a hireling. But the Chief Shepherd restored Peter. The exchange wasn't easy, but Peter was gifted with his life's commission: "Tend my sheep." And so here, so many years past that painful encounter, Peter speaks to those under his mentorship, and he passes on the commission: "Be shepherds of God's flock." Peter had gotten it straight. Anyone who serves the kingdom serves at the pleasure of the Chief Shepherd. The burden can be heavy, but the reward is . . . priceless.

Day 4: A Psalm

First Contact

According to Merriam-Webster, a *refuge* is: (1) a shelter or protection from danger or distress; (2) a place that provides shelter or protection; (3) something to which one has recourse in difficulty. What a refuge is *not* is an antidote for trouble. I picture a cave in the face of a cliff. The climber has found a place that is dry and safe, a place where he can strip off sodden, cold clothes and build a fire to get him through the night. But the storm continues to rage. A refuge does not necessarily stop the storm; it just gives you a safe place to rest.

Read through Psalm 11 once (preferably out loud) without stopping to take notes. Then follow the instructions in Reading & Observing in your second reading.

Psalm 11
For the director of music. Of David.

¹ In the LORD I take refuge.
    How then can you say to me:
    "Flee like a bird to your mountain.
² For look, the wicked bend their bows;
    they set their arrows against the strings
to shoot from the shadows
    at the upright in heart
³ When the foundations are being destroyed,
    what can the righteous do?"
⁴ The LORD is in his holy temple;
    the LORD is on his heavenly throne.

He observes everyone on earth;
    his eyes examine them.
⁵ The LORD examines the righteous,
    but the wicked, those who love violence,
    he hates with a passion.
⁶ On the wicked he will rain
    fiery coals and burning sulfur;
    a scorching wind will be their lot.
⁷ For the LORD is righteous,
    he loves justice;
    the upright will see his face.

Reading & Observing

Read through the psalm again, this time looking for these things:

○ Which collection does the psalm belong to (Book I, II, III, IV, V)?

○ Is there a superscript? If so, what is it? Who is the psalm attributed to?

○ What type of psalm is it? (What is the psalmist doing: praying, praising, complaining, giving thanks, etc.?)

○ Is the psalmist in trouble?

○ What advice is given to him regarding his situation?

○ How does he refute that advice?

○ Where does he place his confidence? Why?

○ What does he conclude?

Responding

○ Sing the psalm! Go to **http://psalms.seedbed.com/** and navigate your way to Psalm 11. Choose one (or all!) of the tune options there and sing this psalm to the Lord.

○ Illustrate the psalm! There are pages set aside at the back of the book (page 209–217) for you to create your own illuminated psalms as well as a sample to get your creative juices flowing.

○ Pray the psalm! Put in your own names and places, and let the ancients pray with you!

○ Choose one paragraph of this psalm to memorize.

○ Set this psalm to your own music. Let the words find their way into your heart.

> Tips to Memorizing
> ○ Start small
> ○ Write it down
> ○ Say it out loud
> ○ Repeat

SESSION 6

Lord, Like a Shepherd Lead Us

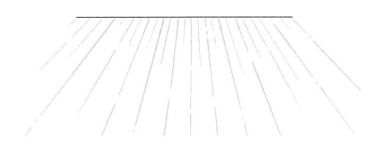

SESSION 6: GROUP MEETING

Schedule

GROUP MEETING
Session 6 Video Teaching and Discussion

INDIVIDUAL STUDY
Day 1: The Form
Day 2: The Exile
Day 3: The Return
Day 4: A Psalm

Debrief & Discover

Ask your group members to tell you everything they know about sheep.

Has anyone in your group ever farmed sheep?

How about goats? Have them share their experience.

Watch Session 6 Video:
LORD, LIKE A SHEPHERD LEAD US
(26 minutes)

Video Notes

These are provided for you and your group members to follow along during the video as well as to offer room for note taking (writing down questions and aha moments as you like).

I. **Psalm 23: Why the image of sheep and shepherds?**

    A. **The symbol of a shepherd in the ancient world**

    B. **Flocks in the ancient world**

       1. **Fat-tailed Awassi sheep**

       2. **Black Sinai goats**

       3. **Why the mixed flock?**

II. Observations about sheep and shepherds

    A. Tim Laniak's observations

    B. What sheep need

    C. Story of Said

III. David as shepherd

    A. 2 Samuel 7

    B. 2 Samuel 12

    C. Psalm 78:70–72

IV. Ezekiel's shepherds (Ezek 34)

    A. Bad shepherds

    B. Good shepherds

V. Jesus as the ultimate Shepherd

    A. Luke 19:10

    B. Matthew 9:36

    C. John 10:11, 14

    D. Matthew 26:31

VI.   The final sheep metaphor: Revelation 7:16–17

VII.   Psalm 23 Richter's translation

Dialogue, Digest & Do

❍ What is something you've learned about sheep and shepherds that is new to you?

❍ In your study guides this week, you were asked to write a job description of a good shepherd. Ask if anyone would be willing to share what they wrote.

❍ What does it mean to have the Lord as our shepherd and for us to be "the sheep of his hand"?

❍ In what ways are sheep and shepherds relevant today? Which do you relate to most?

❍ Do you consider it easier to be led or to lead? Why? How does this effect your relationship with Jesus?

❍ How was Jesus both a shepherd and a lamb at the same time? Why do you think this is?

❍ Sandy talks about shepherds also being sheep, and that even shepherds need to be lead, defended, and directed. Are you resting in the Great Shepherd's care? In what ways?

Next Week

We've all been hurt. We've all experienced loss. We've all gone through things that we don't understand. We're not alone. Next week we'll look at the largest single category of literature in the Psalms—the lament.

Closing Prayer

Ask your group members if there is anything they would like prayer for—especially something highlighted by this week's video.

Reminder: If you are behind in the reading, pick up with the individual study tomorrow to get back on track.

SESSION 6: INDIVIDUAL STUDY

The Anatomy of Lament

A Word from Sandy

In our lesson this week I tell the story of Israel's exile. I speak of it as the darkest day in all Israelite history. This is the moment when all the rebellion and distraction and complacency of God's people come home to roost, and the axe is laid to the root of the tree. A broken covenant, a broken dream, a broken people. Typically, by the time biblical history reaches the exile, Christians have lost interest. But the exile is in reality the great watershed of Israelite history and cannot be sidelined. The study in Ezekiel we did in individual study five embodies this moment—the shepherds have failed, the flock is scattered, and the wolves are circling. Nebuchadnezzar and his armies win the day. Jerusalem is razed, the temple which has housed the sweet songs of the Psalter for centuries is burned and looted, and the children of Abraham lie slain in the streets. If there was ever a day for lament, this is it.

As I state in the video, "Everything he [the prophet Jeremiah] has invested his life in has been dragged away by his enemy . . . and he grieves." Jeremiah's grief has been preserved in the book of Lamentations—his public lament over the destruction of his city and the failure of his people. Have you ever found yourself in Jeremiah's space? Where you've watched the work of your life go up in smoke? When the family business fails, the marriage collapses, the church splits, the child is alienated? Sometimes it happens because bad stuff is everywhere; sometimes it happens because we've blown it. For Israel, on July 18, 586 BCE, they were agonizingly aware that what was happening . . . was their own stupid fault.

Real Time & Space

A lament, a psalm of complaint, can be either individual or communal. Whereas the communal lament names a grief the entire community is experiencing, acknowledges the failure of the community, and cries out to God in unison for deliverance, an individual lament is one believer against the storm. LaSor, Hubbard, and

Bush state that most typically an individual lament is written in response to social persecution or exclusion and illness.[40]

What I find so interesting about this is that these are still two of the most painful things that can happen to a human being: finding yourself isolated from your community, and having your body fail you. But whereas we are allowed to ask for help with the second—announce it during "prayer request" time, post about the details of our treatment on social media—the former is a source of shame. We are *not* allowed to talk about being excluded by the "insider" families at church or the fact that our sweet Southern girl did not receive an invitation to the debutante ball. We do *not* announce that our boss passed us over for promotion for a more politically savvy colleague. And we for sure do not post on social media when we're being investigated at work for potentially discriminatory behavior or that our daughter is struggling with depression because of an abortion. The "knocked the wind out of me" pain and injustice of all these events are equally real, but whereas some of them we get to share with the community, the others we hide. This is where the power of the lament comes into play.

The lament psalm will begin with (1) an address of praise to God for his mighty acts in the past. Next comes (2) the complaint in distress, (3) a protest of innocence, (4) a petition for deliverance, and finally, a lament will *always* conclude with (5) a declaration of confidence in God's good character and a vow to praise him, regardless of the current crisis. These literary features may be mixed and matched as the psalmist wishes, but each will be found in every lament uttered in the book of Psalms (see box below and on page 161).

The use of community laments is illustrated in the narrative portions of our Bibles. Two examples of community laments include Solomon's dedication of the temple in 1 Kings 8, which details occasions when God's people would gather to pray for deliverance (1 Kgs 8:33–40), and Joel's summons to his people to assemble, fast, and beg for deliverance from a locust plague (Joel 2:15–17). Individual laments, as mentioned above, often focus on social persecution (unjust accusation and resulting abandonment by friends; see Pss 3, 5, 7, and 17 as examples) and illness (see Pss 38, 39, 62, and 88). LaSor, Hubbard, and Bush say it this way: "Thanksgiving for the past, rededication for the present, and expectation for the future were the all-embracing components of Israel's worship as voiced in the Psalms—a worship rooted in the healing, compelling, and hopeful revelation of God in their history."[41]

---

[40] LaSor, Hubbard, and Bush, *Old Testament Survey*, 438.
[41] LaSor, Hubbard, and Bush, *Old Testament Survey*, 443.

Form of a Lament [42]

A. Address to God: Long or short, this section speaks to God's mighty acts in the past as the foundation for the appeal to come.

B. Complaint
   a. In community laments, the issue might be a military crisis, drought, famine, or plague.
   b. In an individual lament, the problem is typically illness or social persecution. Hence, we will hear a lot about enemies, fear, death, sometimes a profound sense of personal sin.

C. Protestation of innocence and/or a plea for forgiveness

D. Confession of trust
   a. The psalmist will announce that they know that God has got this.
   b. Often launches with the word *but* or *nevertheless* in your Bible.

E. Petition: The psalmist names one's need, begging God to intervene and deliver the suppliant from the dangers at hand.

F. Words of assurance
   a. God speaks, assuring the suppliant or the congregation of his ability to act (cf. Ps 12:5).
   b, Some theorize that in congregational settings these words were actually spoken by the priest or perhaps the prophet.

G. Vow to Praise: The worshiper now declares/swears that they will call upon the God of Israel, testify to his mighty deeds publicly, and often offers a final exclamation of praise.

---

[42] Anderson, *Out of the Depths*, 76–77.

Day 1: The Form

First Contact

Do you remember that exercise in middle school when you were asked to write a haiku, a limerick, and a sonnet? Your English teacher handed out a set of instructions and a sample and you went at it. For me (and my cluster of desks), the first attempts were laughable, but the exercise had merit. I found myself learning to appreciate the creative energy of having to adapt to a form, and the pedagogical impact of recognizing a form. Thus, for your reading pleasure, a limerick.

There was a young girl on a tower.
Who looked just as fresh as a flower.
Her hair was like silk,
Her skin smooth as milk,
But her breath made the strongest knight cower.[43]

Into the Book

As detailed above, every lament psalm in our Bibles has a "form." The form has *structure* and *function*. The structure gives the psalmist a scaffolding within which to compose his psalm and express himself. The function gives the lament a *place* in public worship. Thus we are looking for (1) an address of praise, (2) a complaint, (3) a protest of innocence, (4) a petition for deliverance, and (5) a vow to praise God. And we are also looking for a moment in the life of the community that gives rise to this expression of distress.

Read Psalm 44. Is this psalm an individual lament or a community lament? How do you know?

---

[43] Author unknown. https://www.pinterest.com/pin/295619163025662601/.

❍ See if you can identify each part of the psalm. Somehow indicate in the text where each element occurs. We suggest using a color-coded highlighter or colored pencil. First <u>underline</u> the named section above in your chosen color, now use that same color to <u>underline</u> the appropriate section below. You might try bracketing off each part, drawing a line between the parts, etc. . . . whatever works.

Psalm 44

For the director of music. Of the Sons of Korah. A maskil.

1 We have heard it with our ears, O God;
    our ancestors have told us
what you did in their days,
    in days long ago.
2 With your hand you drove out the nations
    and planted our ancestors;
you crushed the peoples
    and made our ancestors flourish.
3 It was not by their sword that they won the
       land,
nor did their arm bring them victory;
it was your right hand, your arm,
    and the light of your face, for you
       loved them.

4 You are my King and my God,
    who decrees victories for Jacob.
5 Through you we push back our enemies;
    through your name we trample our foes.

6 I put no trust in my bow,
    my sword does not bring me victory;
7 but you give us victory over our enemies,
    you put our adversaries to shame.
8 In God we make our boast all day long,
    and we will praise your name forever.

9 But now you have rejected and humbled us;
    you no longer go out with our armies.
10 You made us retreat before the enemy,
    and our adversaries have plundered us.
11 You gave us up to be devoured like sheep
    and have scattered us among the nations.
12 You sold your people for a pittance,
    gaining nothing from their sale.
13 You have made us a reproach to our
       neighbors,
    the scorn and derision of those around us.
14 You have made us a byword among the
       nations;
    the peoples shake their heads at us.
15 I live in disgrace all day long,

and my face is covered with shame
16 at the taunts of those who reproach and
revile me
because of the enemy, who is bent
on revenge.

17 All this came upon us,
though we had not forgotten you;
we had not been false to your covenant.
18 Our hearts had not turned back;
our feet had not strayed from your path.
19 But you crushed us and made us a haunt for
jackals;
you covered us over with deep darkness.

20 If we had forgotten the name of our God
or spread out our hands to a foreign god,

21 would not God have discovered it,
since he knows the secrets of the heart?
22 Yet for your sake we face death all day long
we are considered as sheep to be
slaughtered.
23 Awake, Lord! Why do you sleep?
Rouse yourself! Do not reject us forever.
24 Why do you hide your face
and forget our misery and oppression?

25 We are brought down to the dust;
our bodies cling to the ground.
26 Rise up and help us;
rescue us because of your unfailing love.

○ For what occasion do you think the community of faith might have utilized this psalm?

○ Are there any indicators in the psalm of public or private function?

Real People, Real Places, Real Faith

You might be interested to know that laments are not unique to Israel. The nations surrounding Israel also wrote laments and for similar reasons. For example, the "Prayer of Lamentation to Ishtar" from Babylonia is a psalm to the goddess of love and war, the "Queen of Heaven." In this psalm, which contains the same elements of a lament found in our Bibles—an address of praise, a complaint, a petition for deliverance, and a vow—the psalmist is lamenting over his affliction. He prays for restoration of his "wretched body," his "sickened heart," and his "wretched intestines" so that "he and all who see him may praise and glorify the goddess."[44] Another example is the Sumerian "Lament for Ur."[45] Like Jeremiah, the author is lamenting the conquest and destruction of his city. Ur was the leading city of ancient Sumer (named in Genesis as Abraham's hometown, Gen 11:27–32) conquered by the Elamites in c. 2000 BCE.

How do these laments differ from those found in our Bibles? Worldview for sure. These laments are fundamentally polytheistic. Thus, they assume that no single god has ultimate power and all the gods can be manipulated—either via their own appetites or via magic. Thus, the Babylonian psalm was to be accompanied by a ritual of incantation designed to cast a spell over the evil spirits and thereby deliver the worshiper. Whereas the worldview of our book of Psalms is founded upon the Torah. It was Yahweh who kept his promises to Abraham in his infertility, to Joseph in his betrayal, to David in his persecution, to Ruth in her desperation, to Hezekiah in his military crisis, who was the source of hope and deliverance. And he could not be manipulated. In other words, in the Psalms, deliverance comes from God alone. Moreover, this God was a god of *hesed* (covenant faithfulness) and he could be trusted.

As for the prophet Jeremiah's lamentation over the city of Jerusalem, "[l]aments over destroyed cities and sanctuaries form a distinct literary genre in ancient Mesopotamia, with roots reaching as far back as the early second millennium BCE. The poems collected in the biblical book of Lamentations probably belong to this genre, and they may have been recited at the site of the ruined Temple as part of a ritual of commemoration on designated fast days."[46]

---

[44] You can find the "Prayer of Lamentation to Ishtar" at http://factsanddetails.com/world/cat56/sub402/entry-6058.html#chapter-21.

[45] You can find the "Lament for Ur" at https://etcsl.orinst.ox.ac.uk/cgi-bin/etcsl.cgi?text=t.2.2.2&charenc=j# or https://oi.uchicago.edu/sites/oi.uchicago.edu/files/uploads/shared/docs/as12.pdf.

[46] Cogan, "Into Exile: From the Assyrian Conquest of Israel to the Fall of Babylon," 242–275, here 267.

Our People, Our Places, Our Faith

Are there modern laments? Absolutely! Andrew Peterson has written something of a modern lament entitled "Is He Worthy?" This song is so powerful that I have it on loop on all my playlists. And when I am overcome with the injustices and brokenness of my world, when despair is knocking on my door, I hit play. This song doesn't have *all* the components of a biblical community lament, but it has many. It launches with the liturgist calling out into the silence: "Do you feel the world is broken?" And the congregation responds: "We do." Like any lament, the psalmist goes on to speak of all that is crushing his soul. And the congregation, touched by the same pain and the power of poetry and song, enters in. There is no protestation of innocence here, but there is a profound confession of trust and words of assurance: "Does our God intend to dwell again with us? He does."

Where does hope come from? How can we face today? Tomorrow? The answer flows from a full and hopeful heart. The psalmist (our man, Andrew Peterson) reminds us of who God is, who we are, and in my favorite line of the entire song, what his intent for us is. What happens when the people of God assemble to sing such words in the unison of joined hearts and voices? The people of God are strengthened to stand another day. They are reminded of and reconnected with the hope that all the powers of darkness cannot vanquish. When they *name* their pain together, and they shout their hope, *together,* the echoes of their song reverberate against the darkness. And there is hope.

Life is hard. The news is not always good. Let the people of God not neglect the power of lament.

Look up and listen to Andrew Peterson's "Is He Worthy?" on YouTube.

Day 2: The Exile

First Contact

In the spring of 2017, we announced to our daughters that we were moving . . . again. At that moment we were settled into our 104-year-old home in Wheaton, Illinois, and we were happy. Schools were good. Friends were good. Our fixer-upper had become "ours." We were good. But the vagaries of life and calling had just thrown us a curve ball. Whereas I had announced more than once that I was going to be buried at 315 West Harrison Avenue (translation: "we are not going *anywhere*"), we were now headed to Santa Barbara, California. Now Santa Barbara is not exactly a bad place to be. Most of you would give your eye-teeth to spend a week on our beaches, meandering through the outdoor malls, eating fresh seafood off the wharf. But for my girls, it was exile. They had a place; they had a name; they were known.

But now at the fragile juncture between elementary and junior high, junior and senior high, I was dragging them off to a place they'd never been before. Not only was everything unfamiliar, it seemed that everyone in Southern California was convinced that Wheaton, Illinois ("is that near Boston?") was nothing but a podunk town that *no one* would choose over the exotic beauty of Santa Barbara. But my girls didn't want palm trees and the Pacific; they weren't interested in the Los Padres or eternal summer . . . they just wanted home.

Into the Book

Before turning to the psalms, take a look at 2 Kings 25:1–2, 8–15, 21b.

¹ So in the ninth year of Zedekiah's reign, on the tenth day of the tenth month, Nebuchadnezzar king of Babylon marched against Jerusalem with his whole army. He encamped outside the city and built siege works all around it. ² The city was kept under siege until the eleventh year of King Zedekiah.

⁸ On the seventh day of the fifth month, in the nineteenth year of Nebuchadnezzar king of Babylon, Nebuzaradan commander of the imperial guard, an official of the king of Babylon, came to Jerusalem. ⁹ He set fire to the temple of the Lord, the royal palace and all the houses of Jerusalem. Every important building he burned down. ¹⁰ The whole Babylonian army under the commander of the imperial guard broke down the walls around Jerusalem. ¹¹ Nebuzaradan the commander of the guard carried into exile the people who remained in the city, along with the rest of the populace and those who had deserted to the king of Babylon. 12 But the commander left behind some of the poorest people of the land to work the vineyards and fields.

¹³ The Babylonians broke up the bronze pillars, the movable stands and the bronze Sea that were at the temple of the Lord and they carried the bronze to Babylon. ¹⁴ They also took away the pots, shovels, wick trimmers, dishes and all the bronze articles used in the temple service. ¹⁵ The commander of the imperial guard took away the censers and sprinkling bowls—all that were made of pure gold or silver.

²¹So Judah went into captivity, away from her land.

○ Who attacked Jerusalem? How long did the siege last?

○ In the verses above, underline the things the Babylonians did. What did they destroy?

❍ What did they do to the temple? What did they take with them?

❍ Verse 21 sums up the result of the siege of Jerusalem. Where did the captors take the inhabitants of Judah?

Now read

Psalm 137

[1] By the rivers of Babylon we sat and wept
    when we remembered Zion.
[2] There on the poplars
    we hung our harps,
[3] for there our captors asked us for songs,
    our tormentors demanded songs of joy;
    they said, "Sing us one of the songs
        of Zion!"
[4] How can we sing the songs of the LORD
    while in a foreign land?
[5] If I forget you, Jerusalem,
    may my right hand forget its skill.

[6] May my tongue cling to the roof of my mouth
    if I do not remember you,
if I do not consider Jerusalem
    my highest joy.
[7] Remember, LORD, what the Edomites did
    on the day Jerusalem fell.
"Tear it down," they cried,
    "tear it down to its foundations!"
[8] Daughter Babylon, doomed to destruction,
    happy is the one who repays you
    according to what you have done to us.
[9] Happy is the one who seizes your infants
    and dashes them against the rocks.

❍ Who is speaking in this psalm?

❍ Where are they?

❍ What did they long for?

❍ What did they wish upon their enemies?

Real People, Real Places, Real Faith

"So Judah went into captivity, away from her land" (2 Kgs 25:21). If you've done some of our earlier curricula, you'll recall that the northern kingdom of Israel fell to the Assyrian army in 722 BCE, leaving only the southern kingdom of Judah remaining in the land. The beginning of the end of the southern kingdom started with a series of bad choices by the kings of Judah who rebelled against their suzerain—Nebuchadnezzar, the king of Babylon. In 597 BCE, in a show of force, the Babylonians made their way to Jerusalem, and took the king of Judah (Jehoiakin) as well as many of the educators and influencers of the society into exile in Babylon (2 Kgs 24:10–17). Nebuchadnezzar also set up a puppet king—Zedekiah. The idea was that this royal replacement would be loyal to Babylon because he owed his throne to the empire.

But the replacement king eventually chose to rebel as well, and Nebuchadnezzar had had enough. After a three-year siege against Jerusalem, in 586 BCE the Babylonian army set fire to the temple, the palace, and the city. They seized the bronze, silver, and gold. They "carried into exile" the entire populace including those in and outside the city, leaving only some of the poorest to tend the land (2 Kgs 25:8–15). The staggering amount of extrabiblical evidence for the fall of Jerusalem affirms the biblical account. Abraham Faust, in his book *Judah in the Neo-Babylonian Period: The Archaeology of Desolation*, describes post–586 BCE Judah as a "post-collapse society." War and deportation had led to famine, disease, looting and flight, and Faust estimates that the population had declined by more than 70 percent.[47] As a result, local infrastructure and kinship networks collapsed, and in the words of archaeologist Daniel Master, "By the second quarter of the sixth century, most regions of Judah were virtually empty."[48]

Why did all of this happen? Politically, the exile happened because the Babylonians (Israel's secular suzerain) were done with Judah's vacillating political loyalties. Theologically, the exile happened because Yahweh (Israel's ultimate suzerain) had also had enough of Judah's vacillating loyalties. And so as promised in the curses of Deuteronomy 28, Yahweh allowed the armies of Babylon to ravage his nation. In our psalm, the survivors of all this trauma are recognizing their own agency in all this loss and responding with a community lament—they "sat and wept" (Ps 137:1).

---

47 Faust, *Judah in the Neo-Babylonian Period*, 248.
48 Master, "Comments on Obed Lipschits," 31–32.

Our People, Our Places, Our Faith

In the introduction to this week's lesson I asked the question: "Have you ever found yourself in Jeremiah's space? Where you've watched the work of your life go up in smoke?" I stated that sometimes the world crumbles around us because life is simply hard; but sometimes it happens because we've blown it. The exile was indeed Israel's fault—the result of unabated and nonrepentant rebellion against the covenant of Yahweh. And when the ugly story came to a close, they knew it. And oh, the agony of watching your world collapse because of your own selfish stupidity. But these same people are about to learn the lesson of Isaiah 40:1–2: "Comfort, comfort my people, says your God. Speak tenderly to Jerusalem and proclaim to her that her hard service has been completed, that her sin has been paid for, that she has received from the Lord's hand double for all her sins."

In other words, even in that darkest of all spaces, where you know that the agonies around you are the result of your own foolishness, forgiveness and deliverance are real. These are the final messages of any lament: a confession of trust, words of assurance, and a vow to praise. Regardless of how you found yourself in your current crisis, hear the good news of the Gospel reiterated in the prayers of the ancients: "Lord, do not forsake me; do not be far from me, my God. Come quickly to help me, my Lord and my Savior!" (Ps 38:21–22).

Day 3: The Return

First Contact

Do you know that as of December 2020, after nine years of war, more than half the population of Syria has been displaced? More than six and a half million people are internally displaced; more than five and a half million are refugees. Try to imagine that statistic in your own country, your own county, your own church. Families have been torn apart by the chaos of war and flight; children have lost years of education; tens of thousands are living in refugee camps without resources or protection.[49] What kind of impact does this have on a nation? Well, according to "Mental Health Facts on Refugees, Asylum-seekers, & Survivors of Forced Displacement" from the American Psychiatric Association, about one out of three refugees experience high rates of depression, anxiety, and post-traumatic stress disorders.[50] Mental function as simple as planning the next day becomes cloudy in a world where there is no structure or schedule, no predictability. That elusive miracle called "hope" disappears as people lose the capacity to imagine a better future. How do you go about rescuing the hearts and minds of a scattered people?

Into the Book

As we saw in yesterday's study, the Babylonians dragged off the people of Israel to a land far away where they spent years in exile, in a land not their own. In Psalm 74 we hear the pleas of those captives.

Read Psalm 74.

○ As you read the psalm, notice the emotion in the words. What kinds of emotions do you hear?

○ What is the psalmist's request?

---

[49] https://www.savethechildren.org/us/what-we-do/emergency-response/refugee-children-crisis/refugee-stories
[50] Mental-Health-Facts-for-Refugees-1.pdf

Psalm 74

1 O God, why have you rejected us forever?
    Why does your anger smolder against the
        sheep of your pasture?
2 Remember the nation you purchased long
        ago,
    the people of your inheritance, whom you
        redeemed—
    Mount Zion, where you dwelt.
3 Turn your steps toward these everlasting
        ruins,
    all this destruction the enemy has brought
        on the sanctuary.
4 Your foes roared in the place where you met
        with us;
    they set up their standards as signs.
5 They behaved like men wielding axes
    to cut through a thicket of trees.
6 They smashed all the carved paneling
    with their axes and hatchets.
7 They burned your sanctuary to the ground;
    they defiled the dwelling place of your
        Name.
8 They said in their hearts, "We will crush them
        completely!"
    They burned every place where God was
        worshiped in the land.
9 We are given no signs from God;
    no prophets are left,
    and none of us knows how long this will be.
10 How long will the enemy mock you, God?
    Will the foe revile your name forever?
11 Why do you hold back your hand, your right
        hand?
    Take it from the folds of your garment and
        destroy them!
12 But God is my King from long ago;
    he brings salvation on the earth.
13 It was you who split open the sea by your
        power;
    you broke the heads of the monster in the
        waters.
14 It was you who crushed the heads of
        Leviathan
    and gave it as food to the creatures of the
        desert.
15 It was you who opened up springs and
        streams;
    you dried up the ever-flowing rivers.
16 The day is yours, and yours also the night;
    you established the sun and moon.
17 It was you who set all the boundaries of the
        earth;
    you made both summer and winter.
18 Remember how the enemy has mocked you,
        LORD,
    how foolish people have reviled your
        name.
19 Do not hand over the life of your dove to
        wild beasts;
    do not forget the lives of your afflicted
        people forever.

²⁰ Have regard for your covenant,
    because haunts of violence fill the dark
        places of the land.
²¹ Do not let the oppressed retreat in disgrace;
    may the poor and needy praise your name.
²² Rise up, O God, and defend your cause;

remember how fools mock you all
    day long.
²³ Do not ignore the clamor of your
    adversaries,
    the uproar of your enemies, which rises
        continually.

Finally, after 70 years in exile, the Israelites returned "home." Their cries heard, their prayers answered.

Read Psalm 126.

Psalm 126

¹ When the LORD restored the fortunes
        of Zion,
    we were like those who dreamed.
² Our mouths were filled with laughter,
    our tongues with songs of joy.
Then it was said among the nations,
    "The LORD has done great things
        for them."
³ The LORD has done great things for us,
    and we are filled with joy.

⁴ Restore our fortunes, LORD,
    like streams in the Negev.
⁵ Those who sow with tears
    will reap with songs of joy.
⁶ Those who go out weeping,
    carrying seed to sow,
will return with songs of joy,
carrying sheaves with them.

○ What tells you that this is (likely) a psalm regarding the return of the exiles?

○ What emotions are expressed in this psalm? How does this compare/contrast to Psalm 74?

Real People, Real Places, Real Faith

As I teach in *The Epic of Eden: A Christian Entry into the Old Testament*, the progression of covenants in our Bibles is also the progression of the great rescue story. The story begins in Eden and concludes in the New Jerusalem . . . and everything in between is the most amazing rescue story known to human history. How will Yahweh get humanity back into the Garden? How will the relationship be restored? Each step along the way, marked by covenants with Noah, Abraham, Moses, David, and finally Jesus, brings Adam and Eve one step closer to their Creator. With each step the reach of redemption widens, so that whereas under the Mosaic covenant only the children of Abraham are offered salvation, in the New Testament the "people of God" are now every man, woman, and child who is willing to say "yes" to Jesus (Mark 16:16; Rom 5:9–10).

In the New Testament the place of God has been transformed from the promised land to the new heavens and the new earth (John 14:1–4; Rev 21:1–4). In the New Covenant, the Presence is no longer limited to the tabernacle or Solomon's temple; now God "tabernacles among us" (John 1:14), has indwelt the Church (Acts 2), and dwells within every believer (1 Cor 6:19). In the "not yet" the Presence will fully return to the earth such that the Spirit will cover the earth the way the "waters cover the sea" (Isa 11:9).

In Isaiah 44:28 we read about a critical juncture in this great story—Yahweh will forgive his people for their breach of the Mosaic covenant and send a champion named Cyrus to deliver the Jews from exile back to Jerusalem. And how ironic that God speaks of this pagan king as "my shepherd": "He is my shepherd and will accomplish all that I please; he will say of Jerusalem, 'Let it be rebuilt,' and of the temple, 'Let its foundations be laid.'" And so it happened. In 539 BCE Cyrus, the king of the Medo-Persian empire conquered Babylon. And one of his first actions was to announce to the hoards of refugees living in ethnic enclaves throughout his capital city that if they wanted, they could go home. Cyrus issued diplomatic papers allowing free passage to these exiles and returned to each community the appurtenances of their temples—idols, vessels, and other valuables covered with gold and silver.

And so the remnant of Israel, the few that were willing to believe the impossible news and courageous enough for the journey ahead, packed up their lives and headed back to their war-torn, burned down, abandoned homeland. The challenge was immense, but the miracle was more immense. "We were like those who dreamed" the psalmist says (Ps 126:1). After all this time, all this suffering, all this loss Yahweh was bringing them home.

Our People, Our Places, Our Faith

How *do* you go about rescuing the hearts and the minds of a nation? In the story of Israel, we see that God did this by confronting their sin, allowing them to suffer the consequences, and then calling them out from their exile into a new identity and a new covenant. A new creation. God's grand story line of rescue did not actually change, but the people did. And the gift of the Psalms is that we have a front-row seat to hearing the heart of this people change. We hear them remind each other of God's mighty acts: "It was you who split open the sea by your power!" (Ps 74:13); we hear their hearts turn to gratitude and hope: "The LORD has done great things for us, and we are filled with joy" (Ps 126:3).

This motif of rescuing exiles is not limited to the Old Testament. Rather, when we read Hebrews 11:13–16 we find that all the sons of Adam and daughters of Eve living in this fallen world are characterized as aliens, strangers, and exiles.

> [13] "All these people were still living by faith when they died. They did not receive the things promised; they only saw them and welcomed them from a distance admitting that they were foreigners and strangers on earth. [14] People who say such things show that they are looking for a country of their own. [15] If they had been thinking of the country they had left, they would have had opportunity to return. [16] Instead, they were longing for a better country—a heavenly one. Therefore God is not ashamed to be called their God, for he has prepared a city for them." (Heb 11:13–16)

As we will learn more about in the next lesson, you and I are indeed exiles. Not necessarily of the southern kingdom of Judah, but exiles of Eden. Each of us has been catastrophically driven from our true homes. Our relationships have been shattered, our people lost. We long for home. And as any refugee populace, each of us needs our hearts and minds restored. In the story of Israel's return we see the miraculous—of all the stories we know of exile under the Assyrians and the Babylonians, we only know one story of return. May I say that your story is a miracle as well? Of all the stories around you of people displaced, homes lost, and the chaos of conflict—yours is a story of return.

Day 4: A Psalm

First Contact

"Experience is the best teacher," they say. And this time, "they" are right. In our psalm today we are listening to the wise words of someone who has "been there." Our psalmist is announcing that God has indeed delivered him in his time of need and he is encouraging us to have confidence that he will do the same for us. "Taste and see that the Lord is good," he exhorts his reader. "I've been there!" he says, "and it's true!" As a professor I am so aware that there are some things that simply cannot be taught; they have to be "caught." And discipleship into a life of joy, a lifelong posture of a grateful heart, true confidence in a God who *will* show up—these things must be "caught." How blessed we are when we have someone in our lives *showing* us how it's done.

In this case, not only is the psalmist telling us his testimony of God's faithfulness, he has also worked hard to make his psalm accessible and easy to memorize. You can't see it, but this psalm is an acrostic. Each line begins with a sequential letter of the Hebrew alphabet. How fun is that? Only the last line stands apart, and perhaps for good reason: "The Lord will rescue his servants; no one who takes refuge in him will be condemned!"

Read through Psalm 34 once (preferably out loud) without stopping to take notes. Then follow the instructions in Reading & Observing in your second reading.

Psalm 34

Of David. When he pretended to be insane before Abimelek, who drove him away, and he left.

¹ I will extol the LORD at all times;
    his praise will always be on my lips.
² I will glory in the LORD;
    let the afflicted hear and rejoice.
³ Glorify the LORD with me;
    let us exalt his name together.
⁴ I sought the LORD, and he answered me;
    he delivered me from all my fears.
⁵ Those who look to him are radiant;
    their faces are never covered with shame.
⁶ This poor man called, and the LORD
        heard him;
    he saved him out of all his troubles.
⁷ The angel of the LORD encamps around those
        who fear him,
    and he delivers them.
⁸ Taste and see that the LORD is good;
    blessed is the one who takes refuge in him.
⁹ Fear the LORD, you his holy people,
    for those who fear him lack nothing.
¹⁰ The lions may grow weak and hungry,
    but those who seek the LORD lack no good
        thing.
¹¹ Come, my children, listen to me;
    I will teach you the fear of the LORD.

¹² Whoever of you loves life
    and desires to see many good days,
¹³ keep your tongue from evil
    and your lips from telling lies.
¹⁴ Turn from evil and do good;
    seek peace and pursue it.
¹⁵ The eyes of the LORD are on the righteous,
    and his ears are attentive to their cry;
¹⁶ but the face of the LORD is against those who
        do evil,
    to blot out their name from the earth.
¹⁷ The righteous cry out, and the LORD hears
        them;
    he delivers them from all their troubles.
¹⁸ The LORD is close to the brokenhearted
    and saves those who are crushed in spirit.
¹⁹ The righteous person may have many
        troubles,
    but the LORD delivers him from them all;
²⁰ he protects all his bones,
    not one of them will be broken.
²¹ Evil will slay the wicked;
    the foes of the righteous will be
        condemned.
²² The LORD will rescue his servants;
    no one who takes refuge in him will be
        condemned.

Reading & Observing

Read through the psalm again, this time looking for these things:

○ Which collection does the psalm belong to (Book I, II, III, IV, V)?

○ Is there a superscript? If so, what is it? Who is the psalm attributed to?

○ What type of psalm is it? (What is the psalmist doing: praying, praising, complaining, giving thanks, etc.?)

○ Is the psalmist in trouble?

○ In verses 1–3, what is the psalmist's intent?

○ What reasons does the psalmist provide for his intent (vv. 4–6)? In other words, what did God do for the psalmist?

○ Do you notice a shift beginning in verse 7? What is the psalmist doing beginning in verse 7 through the remainder of the psalm?

○ Highlight the instructions the psalmist gives his listeners.

○ Circle the benefits provided to the one who obeys his instructions.

Responding

What should our response be when God answers our prayers? As the psalmist shows us, our response should be to thank God and to proclaim his greatness!

○ Sing the psalm. Go to **http://psalms.seedbed.com/** and navigate your way to Psalm 34 and choose one (or all!) of the tune options there and sing this psalm to the Lord.

○ Illustrate the psalm! There are pages set aside at the back of the book (pages 209–217) for you to create your own illuminated psalms as well as a sample to get your creative juices flowing.

○ Pray the psalm! Put in your own names and places, and let the ancients pray with you!

○ Choose one paragraph of this psalm to memorize.

○ Set this psalm to your own music. Let the words find their way into your heart.

Tips to Memorizing
○ Start small
○ Write it down
○ Say it out loud
○ Repeat

SESSION 7

The Anatomy
of a Lament

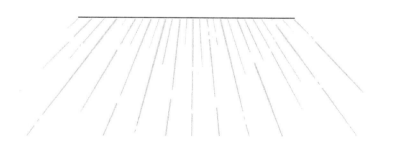

SESSION 7: GROUP MEETING

Schedule

GROUP MEETING

Session 7 Video Teaching and Discussion

INDIVIDUAL STUDY

Day 1: The Choice

Day 2: The Anointing

Day 3: Our Model

Day 4: A Psalm

Debrief & Discover

Ask your group members, "What is a lament?"

Watch Session 7 Video:
THE ANATOMY OF A LAMENT
(25 minutes)

Video Notes

These are provided for you and your group members to follow along during the video as well as to offer room for note taking (writing down questions and aha moments as you like).

I. What is a lament?

    A. Psalms of complaint

    B. Individual

    C. Communal

II. Layout of a lament

    A. Address of praise

    B. Complaint in distress

      C. Protest of innocence

      D. Petition for deliverance

      E. Vow to praise

III.   Examples

      A. Individual lament: Psalm 44

          1.   Address of praise

          2.   Complaint in distress

          3.   Protestation of innocence

          4.   Petition for deliverance

          5.   Promise to praise

      B. Community lament: The book of Lamentations

      C. Psalm 62

Dialogue, Digest & Do

❍ Sandy states that the lament is the largest single category of literature in the book of Psalms, and that there are more individual laments than any other genre of psalm. Do you find that surprising? Why or why not?

❍ Review the standard format of the lament with your group.

❍ Why is it that we find more laments than any other category in the Psalms?

❍ Did you realize before now that the book of Lamentations is actually a "lament"? How does knowing that and the story of Jeremiah and the exile impact you?

❍ What is something you learned about a lament that has changed your understanding of how and in what ways we communicate with God personally and deeply?

Sandy referred to Andrew Peterson's song "Is He Worthy?" in the homework this past week. "What happens when the people of God assemble to sing such words in the unison of joined hearts and voices? The people of God are strengthened to stand another day. They are reminded of and reconnected with the hope that all the powers of darkness cannot vanquish the light. When they name their pain together, and they shout their hope together, the echoes of their song reverberate against the darkness. And there is hope." Take a few minutes to look up "Is He Worthy?" on YouTube. Listen as a group and respond.

Next Week

How are you doing on memorizing those psalms? We have one more week to go. Next week is our final session and we get to talk about . . . you guessed it . . . Jesus!

Closing Prayer

Ask your group members if there is anything they would like prayer for—especially something highlighted by this week's video.

Reminder: If you are behind in the reading, pick up with the individual study tomorrow to get back on track.

SESSION 7: INDIVIDUAL STUDY

Jesus and the Psalms

A Word from Sandy

You did it! You've made it to the last lesson in the study, and this one is all about Jesus! Thank you for joining me on this journey into and through the psalms. It has been my distinct pleasure and joy to be your guide! My prayer remains that from this experience your own prayers and praises have been transformed and more deeply connected to the practice of the worshipers of old.

As we've already noted, the book of Psalms is the most quoted Old Testament book in the New Testament. Why? Most would argue that the first-century Jewish community was looking to the Psalms to answer the biggest question of their day: "Is Messiah coming? And if so, who will he be?" Why might the first-century believers think that the book of Psalms contained that information? Because it was "David's Book." And Israel's Messiah must be a son of David. So they were "searching the Scriptures"—specifically David's book—to find David's heir. As a result, the Psalms are all over the New Testament. And two of them are extremely strategic to the Gospel story as they mark the beginning and the end of Jesus's ministry: Psalm 2 and Psalm 22. These two psalms will shape our last lesson together, "Jesus and the Psalms."

As is always our practice, we will begin our study with the function of these psalms in their Old Testament context. We'll remember from way back in session one that Psalm 2 was placed at the beginning of the hymn-book of Israel in order to shape the lens of the reader. Whereas the first psalm directs the reader toward the Torah—the foundation of our faith, the law and covenant of Israel, Psalm 2 sets our lens by casting our vision toward the culmination of the great story—the consummation of our faith, the hope of Messiah's kingdom. In session five we also discovered that this psalm was used in the coronation rituals of the Israelite kings . . . another reason it will have such a high profile in the Gospels!

Our second "Jesus psalm" is Psalm 22, an individual lament. In the Gospels this psalm makes its appearance at the end of Jesus's life—specifically during the passion narrative. Also a Psalm of David, it begins with the standard *cry of distress*, moves on to an *expression of trust, lament, prayer of confidence* and all the other elements we have come to expect from a lament. As we study this psalm this week you will recognize an array of narrative details that appear in the story of Christ's trial, torture, and crucifixion. Indeed, as some have noted, it seems that Mark is utilizing Psalm 22 almost as a script for his telling of the tale.

Real Time & Space

When Nehemiah prayed for God to bless his mission to bring a second wave of exiles home to Jerusalem in 445 BCE, he prayed: "Remember the instruction you gave your servant Moses, saying, 'If you are unfaithful, I will scatter you among the nations, but if you return to me and obey my commands, then even if your exiled people (literally "scattered ones") are at the farthest horizon (literally "the edge of heaven"), I will gather them from there and bring them to the place I have chosen as a dwelling for My name'" (Richter based on NIV, Neh 1:8–9). Do you hear the "flock" language here? Nehemiah is calling on the great Shepherd to seek and save the lost. Who are the lost? In Nehemiah's prayer, they are the exiles. His dream? To restore the nation of Israel, under the aegis of a son of David, to rebuild the temple and restore the Presence to the community of faith.

We should be interested in the fact that Nehemiah stands nearly a hundred years behind Ezra and the *first* wave of returning exiles, but he is still praying for restoration. A quick trip through the Intertestamental literature shows us that even *after* the Jews returned, and *after* the temple had been rebuilt, the leaders of the Jewish community continued to pray for the same. The writer of 2 Maccabees 1:27–29 prays, "Gather those together that are scattered from us, deliver them that serve among the heathen, look upon them that are despised and abhorred, and let the heathen know that you are our God. . . . Plant your people again in your holy place, as Moses has spoken." Baruch, a scribe of Jeremiah, adds the prayer: "Arise, O Jerusalem, and stand on high, and look about toward the east, and behold your children gathered from the west to the east by the word of the Holy One, rejoicing in the remembrance of God. For they departed from you on foot, and were led away by their enemies, but God brings them to you exalted with glory, as children of the kingdom" (Bar 5:55).

So even in the days well after the return, the Jewish community continues to pray for restoration. Why? Because the kingdom had not yet come. Yes, the "remnant" had returned and rebuilt Jerusalem, but there were many exiles of the northern and southern kingdoms still out there. Meanwhile, those repatriated to the land of Israel/Palestine were living as subjects of first Persia, then Greece, then Rome. And they were suffering. What is the great hope of their prayers? That God will raise up for them their king, the son of David, who will deliver them from the Gentiles, and lead them in obedience to God's covenant. In our next lesson we will see how the Psalms play a role in the Gospel writers' identification of Jesus as this king, the one who will truly gather the scattered ones of Israel.

Day 1: The Choice

First Contact

When a country moves from one ruler to the next, it is typically a time of great national insecurity. As I write this, election day 2020 in the United States has just passed. The lead-up to this election has seen bitterly divided parties, polarization of the media, an unprecedented level of mistrust from the populace, and a hotly contested election process. This transition from one national leader to the next has been the most contested of my lifetime by far. But one of the gifts of American democracy is that even with this kind of conflict, outright violence is very unusual and decried by both parties. Not so in the military coups so common to global history and still known in hot spots all over our planet. An existing government is forced from power, violence ensues, a new political faction seizes power and the populace is thrown into (often bloody) chaos. Psalm 2 describes just such a potential scenario. In *Performing the Psalms*, Ronald Cox describes it this way: "The Psalm is a dramatic description of the chaos that ensues at the transition from one ruler to another and of the sovereignty of God that stands against and vanquishes the chaos."[51]

Into the Story

We have already looked a bit at Psalm 2 earlier in our study (see individual study three, day two). Let's revisit this one on the next page.

---

[51] Cox, *Performing the Psalms*, 96.

Psalm 2

1 Why do the nations conspire
   and the peoples plot in vain?
2 The kings of the earth rise up
   and the rulers band together
   against the LORD and against his anointed,
      saying,
3 "Let us break their chains
   and throw off their shackles."
4 The One enthroned in heaven laughs;
   the LORD scoffs at them.
5 He rebukes them in his anger
   and terrifies them in his wrath, saying,
6 "I have installed my king
   on Zion, my holy mountain."
7 I will proclaim the LORD's decree:

He said to me, "You are my son;
   today I have become your father.
8 Ask me,
   and I will make the nations your inheritance,
   the ends of the earth your possession.
9 You will break them with a rod of iron;
   you will dash them to pieces like pottery."
10 Therefore, you kings, be wise;
   be warned, you rulers of the earth.
11 Serve the LORD with fear
   and celebrate his rule with trembling.
12 Kiss his son, or he will be angry
   and your way will lead to your destruction,
for his wrath can flare up in a moment.
   Blessed are all who take refuge in him.

○ Who is speaking in verse 3 and what do they intend to do?

○ What kind of language is found in verse 3? (If you've done previous Epic of Eden studies, think back to Isaiah.)

○ Who is speaking in verse 6 and what has he done?

○ Who is "proclaiming the LORD's decree" in verses 7–12?

○ What is the meaning of these words in verse 7: "You are my son; today I have become your father"?

○ What is the warning found in the closing verses?

Real People, Real Places, Real Faith

Adoption in the ancient Near East was vastly different than adoption today. Today the whole process can take months, even years. It nearly always involves children, and there are dozens of professionals superintending the process. In the ancient Near East, however, the process was much simpler. If a man wanted to adopt a son (typically an adult heir), he would go to the village square and, in front of a town official and several witnesses, say just this: "Today I am adopting so-and-so, he is my son. I am his father."[52] That's it. The announcement would then be recorded, and the adoptee became the man's heir.

What we see in Psalm 2 is the standard adoption formula—completely recognizable to an ancient audience. But what is happening in Psalm 2 is not exactly a standard adoption. Rather, the human king is being recognized and approved by Yahweh as his heir, which means that the human king is being moved to a higher caste. This "adoption" transforms the Davidic king into the mediator between the divine and human realm, offers him God-given authority, and makes the king the steward over the deity's landholdings (in Israel that would be the promised land). The human king's responsibility was therefore to defend those landholdings and manage them wisely. Essentially, Yahweh is announcing this human king as his chosen vassal. And whereas in Mesopotamia and Egypt such an adoption might be interpreted as transforming the human king into deity, that was not the case in Israel.

Reference to an another ancient Near Eastern practice appears in verse 9. What does "dash them to pieces like pottery" mean? Some suggest this may be a reference to an execration ritual found in Middle Kingdom Egyptian execration texts.[53] In an attempt to prevent rebellious actions against the king, magic was deployed. The name of the enemy would be written on a small clay statue (think voodoo doll). Then the pottery would be tied up, "smashed, stomped, stabbed, speared, spat on, locked in a box, burned," and urinated on for good measure! One such text instructs the cult practitioner to spit on the statue four times, trample it, strike it with a spear, pierce it with a knife, put what remains in the fire, and then spit in the fire as many times as he can![54]

---

52   The Code of Hammurapi (§§170–171) contains a law concerning social rank within a family which provides us with some information regarding the adoption process. In this law, we see similar language to that found in our psalm. "If a man's first chosen wife bore him sons and his slave woman (also) bore him sons (and if) the father during his lifetime has declared to the sons whom the slave woman bore him: '(You are) my sons' (and thereby) he has counted them alongside the sons of the first chosen wife . . ." (Samuel Greengus, *Laws in the Bible and in Early Rabbinic Collections* [Eugene, OR: Cascade, 2011], 77–78, emphasis added).

53   Hilber, *Royal Psalms in Cultic Prophecy in the Psalms*, 99.

54   Kerry Muhlestein, "Execration Ritual," *UCLA Encyclopedia of Egyptology*, https://escholarship.org/uc/item/3f6268zf

And what of the words "Kiss his son" (Ps 2:12)? As discussed in the video, we have many pictorial presentations coming out of the ancient Near East where a vassal or conquered king shows his loyalty to his overlord by kissing him—specifically, abasing himself on the ground and kissing his overlord's feet. And so in our psalm, Yahweh is commanding *his* vassals (the royalty of Israel and the kings of the surrounding nations) to recognize that Yahweh has appointed his king and to respond appropriately. The anointed one of Yahweh carries Yahweh's authority, and any human leader who fails to recognize that will pay the consequences.

Our People, Our Places, Our Faith

As we translate kings and kingdoms, armies and battles into our current faith world, let me remind you of the great Story. Indeed, 1 Corinthians 15 speaks of the last battle, of the last king, over the last enemy. The opponent in this battle? Death. The apostle tells us that there is already a strategy laid out for this final contest between the Creator and the forces that have sought to challenge his sovereignty.

First, Christ will come. "[24] Then the end will come, when he hands over the kingdom to God the Father after he has destroyed all dominion, authority and power. [25] For he must reign until he has put all his enemies under his feet. [26] The last enemy to be destroyed is death. [27] For he 'has put everything under his feet.' Now when it says that 'everything' has been put under him, it is clear that this does not include God himself, who put everything under Christ. [28] When he has done this, then the Son himself will be made subject to him who put everything under him, so that God may be all in all." The results of this last battle are further described in Revelation 21:1–4 (one of my favorite passages in all the Bible): "Then I saw 'a new heaven and a new earth,' for the first heaven and the first earth had passed away, and there was no longer any sea. I saw the Holy City, the new Jerusalem, coming down out of heaven from God, prepared as a bride beautifully dressed for her husband. And I heard a loud voice from the throne saying, 'Look! God's dwelling place is now among the people, and he will dwell with them. They will be his people, and God himself will be with them and be their God. He will wipe every tear from their eyes. There will be no more death or mourning or crying or pain, for the old order of things has passed away.'"

More than likely you lost focus before you reached the final verses here. Mostly because the images and metaphors are not familiar. Might this scene be more recognizable if described by the patron saint of evangelicalism, the inimitable C. S. Lewis? Try these images. In the final lines of his *The Last Battle,* after the "good guys" shared victory over evil Rishda Tarkaan, Aslan clues the children into the great story they had been part of all along. He tells them that the Narnia they had known and loved, the Narnia so often threatened by those who would imprison or destroy it, was not the *real* Narnia. "That had a beginning and an end. It was only a shadow or a copy of the real Narnia which has always been here and always will be here: . . . You need not mourn over Narnia, Lucy. All of the old Narnia that mattered, all the dear creatures, have been drawn into the real Narnia through the Door. . . . The term is over: the holidays have begun. The dream is ended: this is the morning."[55] Yes, kings and kingdoms, armies and wars might not seem relevant to our current faith world, but that is only because our vision is too narrow. There is a king and a battle that must be won. Every citizen of every nation must indeed "kiss the Son" because he will indeed win this war . . . and the morning will begin.

---

[55] Lewis, *The Complete Chronicles of Narnia*, 519, 523.

Day 2: The Anointing

First Contact

Have you ever heard of "the Chosen One trope"? In literature, a trope is simply a common convention, anything that gets used often enough to be recognized. So "the Chosen One trope" occupies a standard plot line that rehearses an unlikely hero burdened with an impossible task for which he was destined from birth. A humble and unlikely leader who courageously embraces the quest necessary to the salvation of his people. A child with a destiny that outstrips his age or resources. Arthur of Camelot, Aragorn son of Arathorn, Morgan the Riddlemaster of Hed, Harry Potter, Percy Jackson, and Moana are all examples of this oft' deployed character. According to the experts, this trope predates the genre of fantasy and even literature itself, and it pops up in every literary medium known to man. Why might that be? Well, perhaps it is because the human heart intuitively longs for a savior, who has no flaws, who humbly and courageously embraces his mission, and who is able to deliver humankind from the forces of evil.

Into the Story

As we enter the Gospel story, every heart and mind is searching for the same thing. Or should I say the same person? Every one of the offspring of Israel knows that the only hope for deliverance, a true return from the exile, the restoration of the kingdom is a righteous son of David.

Read Matthew 1:1; 3:1–17.

[1:1] **This is the genealogy of Jesus the Messiah the son of David, the son of Abraham.**

[3:1] **In those days John the Baptist came, preaching in the wilderness of Judea** [2] **and saying, "Repent, for the kingdom of heaven has come near."** [3] **This is he who was spoken of through the prophet Isaiah:**

"A voice of one calling in the wilderness,

'Prepare the way for the Lord,

make straight paths for him.'"

[4] John's clothes were made of camel's hair, and he had a leather belt around his waist. His food was locusts and wild honey. [5] People went out to him from Jerusalem and all Judea and the whole region of the Jordan. [6] Confessing their sins, they were baptized by him in the Jordan River.

[7] But when he saw many of the Pharisees and Sadducees coming to where he was baptizing, he said to them: "You brood of vipers! Who warned you to flee from the coming wrath? [8] Produce fruit in keeping with repentance. [9] And do not think you can say to yourselves, 'We have Abraham as our father.' I tell you that out of these stones God can raise up children for Abraham. [10] The ax is already at the root of the trees, and every tree that does not produce good fruit will be cut down and thrown into the fire.

[11] "I baptize you with water for repentance. But after me comes one who is more powerful than I, whose sandals I am not worthy to carry. He will baptize you with the Holy Spirit and fire. [12] His winnowing fork is in his hand, and he will clear his threshing floor, gathering his wheat into the barn and burning up the chaff with unquenchable fire."

[13] Then Jesus came from Galilee to the Jordan to be baptized by John. [14] But John tried to deter him, saying, "I need to be baptized by you, and do you come to me?"

[15] Jesus replied, "Let it be so now; it is proper for us to do this to fulfill all righteousness." Then John consented.

[16] As soon as Jesus was baptized, he went up out of the water. At that moment heaven was opened, and he saw the Spirit of God descending like a dove and alighting on him. [17] And a voice from heaven said, "This is my Son, whom I love; with him I am well pleased."

❍ How is Jesus described in Matthew 1:1?

❍ Compare Jesus's genealogy with that of his forefather David in Ruth 4:17–22 and his fore-forefather Abraham in Genesis 11:10–26. Notice whose name comes first in each of these. What does the primacy of names/naming tell you?

○ How is John the Baptist described in Matthew 3:1–6?

○ Let's start with John's appearance. What do you think of his fashion and dietary choices?

○ In verses 6–7 we learn that John has chosen the wilderness as his pulpit, and that he is "baptizing" people. Remembering that the New Testament hasn't been written yet, so "Christian" baptism doesn't exist yet, what in the world is John doing? (Do a search on the term *mikveh* if you're interested in going further.)

○ Why do you think the urban elite of Jerusalem would schlep all the way out to the wilderness to hear John preach?

○ What do you know about the Pharisees and Sadducees? Do a quick Google search and bring some information back to your group.

○ The Pharisees and Sadducees are supposed to be "holy men." What do you think has gone wrong here?

○ Matthew 3:3 in your Bible should refer you back to Isaiah 40:3 (from where the Gospel writer pulls his quotation). Flip back and read the quote in context there.

If you've done the *Epic of Eden Isaiah* study, you already know that Isaiah 40 speaks of the restoration of Israel following the exile. Let's read a bit of it.

> ¹⁰ See, the Sovereign LORD comes with power,
>> and he rules with a mighty arm.
> See, his reward is with him,
>> and his recompense accompanies him.
> ¹¹ He tends his flock like a shepherd:
>> He gathers the lambs in his arms
> and carries them close to his heart;
>> he gently leads those that have young.

○ How do these verses relate to the exile's experience and the people's current needs?

○ How might John the Baptist be rehearsing the same message to a similar need?

Take a look at the rest of Isaiah's oracle below:

> ²¹ Do you not know?
>> Have you not heard?
> Has it not been told you from the beginning?
>> Have you not understood since the earth was founded?
> ²² He sits enthroned above the circle of the earth,
>> and its people are like grasshoppers.
> He stretches out the heavens like a canopy,
>> and spreads them out like a tent to live in.
> ²³ He brings princes to naught
>> and reduces the rulers of this world to nothing.

○ Why did Jesus come to John?

○ What happened when Jesus came up out of the water?

○ What did the voice from heaven say? Write it down here.

○ Do you recognize the quotation from Psalm 2? Why would the voice on high use Psalm 2 to speak of Jesus?

○ Turn back to individual study three, day two, and review the 1 Kings passages and questions. In Israel, how were the new kings recognized?

○ What impact would the scene of Jesus's baptism have on the first-century Jews who were awaiting their Messiah? Would they have recognized Jesus as the One?

Real People, Real Places, Real Faith

How do the Gospel writers announce the arrival of the true Messiah, the "Return of the King" (blatant Tolkien reference!)? They do it the same way the nation of Israel had always done it. First, they identify a biological son of David (your exercise in Matthew 1 above) and then they find themselves a prophet. In Israelite practice, the choice of the king was always the task of the prophet. If you've worked through Epic of Eden: Understanding the Old Testament, you know that prophets were the "king-makers" and "king-breakers." Samuel found and anointed Saul according to Yahweh's direction. He then found and removed Saul, anointing David in his place. Nathan will anoint Solomon and announce his identity as Yahweh's choice to the people. This practice will be repeated throughout the Israelite monarchy.

How will this be handled in the New Covenant? Well, first we need to find ourselves a prophet. And Matthew, Mark, Luke, and John do just that by introducing the ministry of Jesus by means of the *last prophet of the old order*: John the Baptist. All of the Gospel writers describe him the very same way: "This is the one referred to by Isaiah the prophet, saying: 'The voice of one crying in the wilderness, make ready the way of the Lord, make his paths straight!'" (See Matt 3:3; Mark 1:3; Luke 3:4; John 1:23.)

As you've seen above, the bucket handle that the Gospel writers are pulling is intended to present the reader with all of Isaiah 40. This is the opening chapter of Isaiah's restoration oracles—the prophet's first word on the restoration of the kingdom! The particular passage (40:3) announces Yahweh's intention to free the exiles of Babylon and bring them home along the same highway that led them into captivity in the first place.

So, what the Gospel writers are telling us by pulling this bucket handle (placing this quotation in John's mouth) is that John the Baptist was the herald of the true restoration of the nation Israel. John is the prophet who announces to the people of Israel that Messiah is here. This is why humble Joseph is greeted in Matthew 1:20 as a "son of David"—a heritage that had probably come to be no more than an embarrassment in his family's current status. This is why it is critical that Jesus be identified as "the King of the Jews" at his crucifixion. This is why there are 12 disciples—the new representatives of the *restored* 12 tribes. This is why John wrote:

> **47 Then the chief priests and the Pharisees called a meeting of the Sanhedrin. "What are we accomplishing?" they asked. "Here is this man performing many signs. 48 If we let him go on like this, everyone will believe in him, and then the Romans will come and take away both our temple and our nation." 49 Then one of them, named Caiaphas, who was high priest that year, spoke up, "You know nothing at all! 50 You do not realize that it is better for you that one man die for the people than that the whole nation perish." 51 He did not say this on his own, but as high priest that year he prophesied that Jesus would die for the Jewish nation, 52 and not only for that nation but also for the scattered children of God, to bring them together and make them one. 53 So from that day on they plotted to take his life. (John 11:47–53)**

This king will not only inherit the nations (Ps 2:8), but he will deliver them.

Our People, Our Places, Our Faith

In Romans 12:2 we read "Do not conform to the pattern of this world, but be transformed by the renewing of your mind. Then you will be able to test and approve what God's will is—his good, pleasing and perfect will." The core idea behind this passage is that there are two kingdoms—one we see, and one we don't. The one we see is shaped by a worldview that is alien to the one we don't. Therefore, the kingdom we *see* is filled with passions and power figures that are equally alien to the kingdom of God. And the more we try to conform our lives to the passions and power of the true kingdom, the more we are going to be in conflict with the kingdom around us. And that is hard.

Shouldn't we be celebrated for being kingdom people? Shouldn't our lives be filled with smooth paths and the praise of our superiors if we embrace the values of God's kingdom? Uh . . . no. "In fact, everyone who wants to live a godly life in Christ Jesus will be persecuted" (2 Tim 3:12) and "blessed are you when people insult you, persecute you and falsely say all kinds of evil against you because of me" (Matt 5:11). Not only is it hard occupying this space, it is *confusing.* Why are people angry at me for doing what we all (should) know is the right thing? Am I wrong? Isn't this what the Bible says?

This conundrum is why those who desire to live godly in Christ Jesus need a regularly scheduled "reality check." What is really real? And the answer is that Yahweh reigns, let the earth rejoice. His value system is the one that is eternal. His definition of good is good. So, when you find yourself in that unenviable spot of having truly sacrificed to do the good and loving thing, and you are finding the "kings of the earth" rising up, and the "rulers" banding together against you, pause for a reality check. "The One enthroned in heaven laughs; he rebukes them in his anger . . . saying, 'I have installed my king on Zion'" (Ps 2:4–6). Your God is strong. Lean in.

Day 3: Our Model

First Contact

It is indeed true that the Fall has made our world Adam's world—with all of the sin and sickness and violence birthed from Adam's rebellion. Therefore "bad" is now built into this profoundly distorted world of ours and violence, poverty, birth defects, and abuse happens. All the time. But for those who have bent the knee to the King of Heaven, our suffering is *never* meaningless. Not only will we will one day be delivered of this present suffering, but our God has promised to weave every thread of our life experience into the tapestry of his plan. More staggering to me is that the essence of the "God with us" promise of the Gospel is that our God actually accompanies us through every moment of our present agony. Yes, "In this world you will have trouble. But take heart! I have overcome the world" (John 16:33).

Into the Story

Yesterday we looked at the beginning of Jesus's ministry. Today we'll look at the end of his ministry, beginning with some telling words from Psalms.

Psalm 22

For the director of music. To the tune of "The Doe of the Morning." A psalm of David.

1 My God, my God, why have you forsaken me?
  Why are you so far from saving me,
  so far from my cries of anguish?
2 My God, I cry out by day, but you do not
    answer,
  by night, but I find no rest.
3 Yet you are enthroned as the Holy One;
  you are the one Israel praises.
4 In you our ancestors put their trust;
  they trusted and you delivered them.
5 To you they cried out and were saved;
  in you they trusted and were not put to
    shame.
6 But I am a worm and not a man,
  scorned by everyone, despised by the
    people.
7 All who see me mock me;
  they hurl insults, shaking their heads.
8 "He trusts in the LORD," they say,
  "let the LORD rescue him.
Let him deliver him,
  since he delights in him."
9 Yet you brought me out of the womb;
  you made me trust in you, even at my
    mother's breast.
10 From birth I was cast on you;
  from my mother's womb you have been
    my God.

11 Do not be far from me,
  for trouble is near
  and there is no one to help.
12 Many bulls surround me;
  strong bulls of Bashan encircle me.
13 Roaring lions that tear their prey
  open their mouths wide against me.
14 I am poured out like water,
  and all my bones are out of joint.
My heart has turned to wax;
  it has melted within me.
15 My mouth is dried up like a potsherd,
  and my tongue sticks to the roof of
    my mouth;
  you lay me in the dust of death.
16 Dogs surround me,
  a pack of villains encircles me;
  they pierce my hands and my feet.
17 All my bones are on display
  people stare and gloat over me.
18 They divide my clothes among them
  and cast lots for my garment.
19 But you, LORD, do not be far from me.
  You are my strength; come quickly to help
    me.
20 Deliver me from the sword,
  my precious life from the power of
    the dogs.
21 Rescue me from the mouth of the lions;
  save me from the horns of the wild oxen.
22 I will declare your name to my people;

in the assembly I will praise you.

²³ You who fear the LORD, praise him!

All you descendants of Jacob, honor him!

Revere him, all you descendants of Israel!

²⁴ For he has not despised or scorned

the suffering of the afflicted one;

he has not hidden his face from him

but has listened to his cry for help.

²⁵ From you comes the theme of my praise in

the great assembly;

before those who fear you I will fulfill my

vows.

²⁶ The poor will eat and be satisfied;

those who seek the LORD will praise him—

may your hearts live forever!

²⁷ All the ends of the earth

will remember and turn to the LORD,

and all the families of the nations

will bow down before him,

²⁸ for dominion belongs to the LORD

and he rules over the nations.

²⁹ All the rich of the earth will feast and

worship

all who go down to the dust will kneel

before him—

those who cannot keep themselves alive.

³⁰ Posterity will serve him;

future generations will be told about the

LORD.

³¹ They will proclaim his righteousness,

declaring to a people yet unborn:

He has done it!

○ What type of psalm is this?

○ To whom is the psalm attributed?

○ Identify the individual parts of the psalm (place brackets around each part, highlight using different colors, draw lines, etc.).

Read Mark 15:1, 15–39.

As you read through this account of Jesus's death, highlight those places where you hear quotes, echoes, or allusions to Psalm 22.

¹ **Very early in the morning, the chief priests, with the elders, the teachers of the law and the whole Sanhedrin, made their plans. So they bound Jesus, led him away and handed him over to Pilate.**

[15] Wanting to satisfy the crowd, Pilate released Barabbas to them. He had Jesus flogged, and handed him over to be crucified.

[16] The soldiers led Jesus away into the palace (that is, the Praetorium) and called together the whole company of soldiers. [17] They put a purple robe on him, then twisted together a crown of thorns and set it on him. [18] And they began to call out to him, "Hail, king of the Jews!" [19] Again and again they struck him on the head with a staff and spit on him. Falling on their knees, they paid homage to him. [20] And when they had mocked him, they took off the purple robe and put his own clothes on him. Then they led him out to crucify him.

[21] A certain man from Cyrene, Simon, the father of Alexander and Rufus, was passing by on his way in from the country, and they forced him to carry the cross. [22] They brought Jesus to the place called Golgotha (which means "the place of the skull"). [23] Then they offered him wine mixed with myrrh, but he did not take it. [24] And they crucified him. Dividing up his clothes, they cast lots to see what each would get.

[25] It was nine in the morning when they crucified him. [26] The written notice of the charge against him read: the KING OF THE JEWS.

[27] They crucified two rebels with him, one on his right and one on his left. [29] Those who passed by hurled insults at him, shaking their heads and saying, "So! You who are going to destroy the temple and build it in three days, [30] come down from the cross and save yourself!" [31] In the same way the chief priests and the teachers of the law mocked him among themselves. "He saved others," they said, "but he can't save himself! [32] Let this Messiah, this king of Israel, come down now from the cross, that we may see and believe." Those crucified with him also heaped insults on him.

[33] At noon, darkness came over the whole land until three in the afternoon. [34] And at three in the afternoon Jesus cried out in a loud voice, *"Eloi, Eloi, lema sabachthani?"* (which means "My God, my God, why have you forsaken me?").

[35] When some of those standing near heard this, they said, "Listen, he's calling Elijah."

[36] Someone ran, filled a sponge with wine vinegar, put it on a staff, and offered it to Jesus to drink. "Now leave him alone. Let's see if Elijah comes to take him down," he said.

[37] With a loud cry, Jesus breathed his last.

[38] The curtain of the temple was torn in two from top to bottom. [39] And when the centurion, who stood there in front of Jesus, saw how he died, he said, "Surely this man was the Son of God!"

❍ Note what stands out to you in your highlights:

Real People, Real Places, Real Faith

Was Jesus's choice of Psalm 22 as his final words another nod to the fact that he was the son of David, the rightful heir to the throne? Or was it more his identification with all of us who have known betrayal, abandonment, humiliation, dehumanization, injustice, collusion, lynching, rape? As we watch Jesus die—stripped, beaten, humiliated—we watch a faithful servant of the Most High in agony. Agony he does not deserve, inflicted by the systemic injustice of a brutal empire, tolerated by a religious elite more concerned with maintaining power than exercising justice. And we can hear in his words that he is also grappling with despair: "Why are you so far from saving me, so far from my cries of anguish?" (v. 1). If ever there was a man who should not have suffered, this is the man. If there was ever a man falsely accused, this is the man. But his innocence changes nothing about his suffering. What it does change . . . is us. You see in the midst of his anguish, Jesus models to us how to not simply endure evil, but to triumph over it. And the darkest moment of his life is transformed into greatest victory.

Now I realize that Jesus is God and the crucifixion can never be duplicated. But please hear again how Jesus deals with his agony. "In you our ancestors put their trust; they trusted and you delivered them. To you they cried out and were saved; in you they trusted and were not put to shame" (Ps 22:4–5). In his blackest night, David's heir, the true king of Israel, our elder brother and the firstborn from the Dead, *models* to us how to navigate the agonies of this life. He prays. To a God who had proved he would not fail. Jesus declares his unending confidence in a God who seems far off. And in his weakest hour, Jesus leans on the faith of those who have gone before. Jesus *lets* the ancients pray for him.

Our People, Our Places, Our Faith

What are *you* facing these days? An injury of the past so severe that you just can't find your way out of the darkness? Betrayal and abandonment, perhaps by the one who promised to "love and cherish until death do us part"? False accusation? Injustice that will not let you up or out? Be comforted, my friend, and set your lens. The kingdom of this world is passing away, and the King of our souls has walked these paths ahead of us . . . and he found strength in the psalms.

Day 4: A Psalm

First Contact

Have you sung the doxology lately? I *love* it acapella with all the great harmonies that people with better talents than me can weave in and out of the melody! The word *doxology* is defined as a short expression of praise to God, often added to the end of longer canticles or hymns. As we've learned, the Psalter includes brief doxologies used to mark the transition from one collection to the next. Similarly, in the Jewish synagogue, some version of the Kaddish (an ancient prayer whose name means most simply "holy" or "sanctify") was used to mark the transition from one section of the service to the next.

Why a doxology for such purposes? What better way to move through a service of worship than to regularly remind ourselves of what God has done, giving thanks for his blessings, and robustly declaring his character to anyone else within earshot? And of course, in a Christian service everyone knows that once the doxology is sung, everyone heads home. Well, I am afraid that is where we find ourselves in our at-home study as well. It is time to sing the doxology of doxologies and mark the end of our deep dive into the book of Psalms. I pray that these words of praise will linger on your lips, bringing joy to your day and light to whatever darkness is creeping in on the edges. Gratitude changes things. So let your gratitude rip today!

Read Psalm 150 once (preferably out loud) without stopping to take notes. Then follow the instructions in Reading & Observing on your second reading.

Psalm 150

¹Praise the LORD.

Praise God in his sanctuary;
    praise him in his mighty heavens.
² Praise him for his acts of power;
    praise him for his surpassing greatness.
³ Praise him with the sounding of the trumpet,
    praise him with the harp and lyre,
⁴ praise him with timbrel and dancing,
    praise him with the strings and pipe,
⁵ praise him with the clash of cymbals,
    praise him with resounding cymbals.
⁶ Let everything that has breath praise
    the LORD.
Praise the LORD.

Reading & Observing

Read through the psalm again, this time looking for these things:

○ To which collection does the psalm belong (Book I, II, III, IV, V)?

○ Is there a superscript? If so, what is it? Who is the psalm attributed to?

○ What type of psalm is it? (What is the psalmist doing: praying, praising, complaining, giving thanks, etc.?)

The psalmist wants the listener to:

○ Do what?

○ To whom?

○ Where?

○ For what reason?

○ With what?

○ By what/whom?

Responding

"Let everything that has breath praise the Lord!"

○ Sing the psalm. Go to **http://psalms.seedbed.com/** and navigate your way to Psalm 150 and choose one (or all!) of the tune options there and sing this psalm to the Lord.

○ Illustrate the psalm! There are pages set aside at the back of the book (page 209–217) for you to create your own illuminated psalms as well as a sample to get your creative juices flowing.

○ Pray the psalm! Put in your own names and places, and let the ancients pray with you!

○ Choose one paragraph of this psalm to memorize.

○ Set this psalm to your own music. Let the words find their way into your heart.

Tips to Memorizing
  ○ Start small
  ○ Write it down
  ○ Say it out loud
  ○ Repeat

My exhortation to you:
    Read the psalms.
    Read them in the morning;
        read them in the evening.
    Read them for their praises;
        read them for their prayers.
    Read them with the words of the psalmist,
        read them with your own words,
    read them with joy,
        read them with tears,
    read them with thanksgiving,
    read them with worship.

Let everyone that has breath read the psalms.

Read the psalms.

SESSION 8

Jesus &
the Psalms

SESSION 8: GROUP MEETING

Schedule

GROUP MEETING

Session 8 Video Teaching and Discussion

Debrief & Discover

Psalms is the most quoted Old Testament book in the New Testament. Ask your members why they think that is.

Watch Session 8 Video:
Jesus & The Psalms
(29 minutes)

Video Notes

These are provided for you and your group members to follow along during the video as well as to offer room for note taking (writing down questions and aha moments as you like).

I.   Psalm 2

    A. The function of Psalm 2 in the Old Testament

        I.   The Messianic psalm (Messiah)

        2.   Coronation rituals (public anointing with oil)

        3.   Yahweh's choice (adoption formula)

            a. 2 Samuel 7

            b. I Samuel 16:7

    B. Psalm 2 in the New Testament

        I.   "Bucket handle" approach

2. Matthew 3

   a. Adoption formula

   b. Public anointing, by the prophet, of the chosen king!

II. Psalm 22

  A. Psalm 22 in the Old Testament

   1. Individual lament

   2. Cry of distress

   3. Expression of trust

   4. Lament

   5. Prayer of confidence

   6. Petition

   7. Vow to praise

  B. Psalm 22 in the New Testament—Mark 15

   1. Individual lament

   2. "My God, my God, why have you forsaken me?"

   3. Jesus dies with the words of the Psalter on his lips

"The Psalms have a unique place in the Bible because [whereas] most of Scripture speaks to us, the Psalms speak for us." (Athanasius)

Dialogue, Digest & Do

○ Psalm 2 has a lot of political themes in it. Is it odd for you to think about God in such a political way? How about the idea of him "scoffing" at the kings of the earth?

○ Talk about the similarities between Psalm 2 and Jesus's baptism. What is the Gospel writer communicating to his audience about who Jesus is?

○ The amount of suffering portrayed in Psalm 22 is hard to handle. Discuss the similarities between Psalm 22 and Jesus's crucifixion.

○ Has anyone in the group seen the movie The Passion? Did they find that difficult to watch? Why or why not?

○ What has been the greatest impact on you through this study? How has your prayer life changed? How has your understanding of the Psalms changed?

Sandy says, "Jesus dies with the words of the Psalter on his lips. . . . The Jesus of the Gospels, in the throes of despair, models to us how to not simply endure, but triumph over, the darkest moments of life. In this blackest of nights, David's heir, the true king of Israel, our elder brother and the firstborn from the Dead . . . prays. He calls out to a God who will not fail. In his weakest hour, he leans on the faith of those who have gone before, and he lets the ancients pray FOR him."

○ It is likely that there are people in your group who have endured real trauma, perhaps trauma they've never shared. Encourage your group members to reframe their suffering within Jesus's suffering. Are there shared experiences? How might this reframing help your group member heal?

○ Challenge each other to commit to reading the Psalms daily and to memorizing a few Psalms.

○ Commit to allow the Psalms to speak for you in your communication with God.

Closing Prayer

In this final group prayer, offer a prayer over your group that each member may elevate his or her own psalms in the tradition set generations ago. Then continue in a revival of committed prayer and praise to the Lord.

Illuminated Psalms

Choose your own Psalm to "illuminate" and draw it on the pages that follow, using this example as your inspiration. Think of each word and its reflection of your prayer or worship as you draw and color. Look up full color illuminated manuscripts for more inspiration.

Psalm _____

Psalm _____

Psalm _____

Psalm _____

Psalm _____

Psalm _____

Psalm _____

Psalm _____

Leader's Guide

This leader's guide is designed for you, the facilitator. If this is a home group, we recommend that an hour and a half be set aside for the video and discussion. If this is a group in a church setting, it can be modified to suit your group's schedule. In a perfect world, we recommend that the leader preview the videos. Outlines for each video session are provided for you and your group members in the Video Notes section in each week of the study.

Keep in mind that curriculum is a tool, not a straitjacket. You are the leader. You are called to lead this group. You need to adjust according to your own style. But we also suggest that group members be allowed to talk, ask questions, offer aloud their aha moments and personal research. These elements are critical to the success of your group. Trust your group members, trust the Bible, trust the Holy Spirit, and let your people talk. Questions are provided to facilitate the discussion.

- ❍ As a reminder, each week the individual homework is on new content, rather than what was taught in the video. Each video teaching is based on the individual study each participant should have done prior to the group meeting session one is unique but gets you on track for session two).

- ❍ Our prayer is that this material will give you the tools you need to successfully facilitate your group in your very own corner of the kingdom. Know that "where two or three are gathered together in my name, there I am with them" (Matt 18:20). And know that the team behind this curriculum is praying daily that wherever you are, the Holy Spirit is with you. Godspeed!

First Things

We are including here a few **suggestions** for the group's introductory meeting. You are welcome to plan this gathering in any way that best suits your group. Let the Holy Spirit be your guide.

○ Make sure that the first gathering offers the group the opportunity to meet each other, get comfortable with one another other, get the curriculum materials in hand, and get *familiar* with those materials.

○ Keep in mind that hospitality is king! Allow the members of the group to briefly introduce themselves (i.e., first name and in one sentence what they hope to gain from this study). If the group is more than seven members, it is often good to have them turn to the person on their right and then on their left and introduce themselves before having everyone introduce themselves to the group as a whole. If this is a new group, know that "adult learning anxiety" is a very real thing. Expressions of hospitality such as snacks, music playing in the background, and a person or two assigned as host or hostess are all extremely helpful to lowering barriers and make the newcomer feel at ease.

○ Pass out materials and explain how the study works. Actually show them the various sections of a day's study. Make sure they are clear that the "homework" is to be completed *before* the video for each week. (The participants should work on individual study one at home prior to viewing the session two video at your next gathering, and so on.)

○ Show your group the streaming video access code on the inside front cover of each study guide. This is a great tool for absences and re-viewing the teaching at any time.

○ As you plan your schedule, it might also be a great thing to set apart a final gathering after the study is complete to debrief and celebrate with some sort of time together as a group.

Practical Tips

○ Choose a **space** for your study that matches the size of your group, facilitates note-taking, and encourages discussion.

○ Have **refreshments**. Lots of studies have shown that adults do way better in small groups when snacks are available. For some reason, having a cup of coffee in their hand makes it easier for adults to speak to the person next to them. And if you pass snack responsibilities around, it gives everyone a chance to get involved.

○ Have someone besides yourself serve as host/hostess (you've got enough to do) and think about having **name tags**. These are very useful for helping folks engage someone they don't really know yet and breaking down barriers.

Each member of your group should receive a copy of ***The Epic of Eden: Psalms Study Guide.*** The guide is intended to provide each participant with "homework" preparing him/her for the next group gathering where the video teaching is presented. *Note:* There is no preparatory work for the first week's video teaching, but from that week forward there is individual homework to be done in the study guide to prepare for the next group meeting and video teaching session.

Each week in the study guide includes **four sets of exercises**—three days of hard study and one bonus psalm study day. Three or four slots of time per week to prepare this homework is a reasonable expectation—not too much, not too little. *Please* communicate to your group members that homework is *not* required.

There will be plenty to do and talk about in the group discussion time following the video teaching each week. This study is intended to help your members enter into inductive study of their Bibles while opening their minds to greater scholarship of the Bible without years of academic classroom work. I've done the heavy lifting and herein pass along the results! My hope is that I've included enough different learning styles that every member of your group will find themselves engaged, challenged. As long as your members feel this way, I've succeeded.

Weekly Group Meeting Line-Up

Debrief & Discover

This section offers a break-the-ice kind of question(s). It intends to get your group thinking and lead into the video for the week.

Watch Session Video (minutes)

Use Streaming Video or DVD. Each video will be approximately 30 minutes. Exact minutes are given in each session.

Dialogue & Digest

This section consists primarily of quotes from the video with questions for discussion based on those quotes. This is also a place for group members to ask questions about the homework and share something from the homework that really captured their attention.

Decide & Do

This is the application section in which the questions are intended to move your group members to some type of action.

Next Week

Here I provide a teaser about what is to come in the next session.

Closing Prayer

This is the time to ask group members if there is anything for which they would like prayer and close the session with prayer.

Format of the Weekly Individual Study Section

○ **A Word from Sandy.** Each week of individual home study commences with the introduction of the topic.

○ **Real Time & Space.** This is a short section that situates the week's study in real time and context.

○ **First Contact.** Each daily study begins with this section designed to get your members thinking about what is to come from their own real time and space.

○ **Into the Book.** This is where the inductive Bible study begins in earnest. Our primary goal is to *lead* your group members into the discovery of the Bible. The questions direct students into a close reading of the text.

○ **Real People, Real Places, Real Faith.** This section provides further information about the original setting of these biblical narratives and characters and challenges your group members to get back into the Bible's real time and space—to put *themselves* into the shoes of these not-so-ivory-tower heroes.

○ **Our People, Our Places, Our Faith.** The final individual study section will bring the ancient story back into a contemporary setting. This exercise will help to teach your members how to responsibly interpret the Bible and transport texts that might have appeared irrelevant into front-and-center relevance for our contemporary contexts.

○ **Reading & Observing.** Day four of individual study begins with reading and observing a psalm.

○ **Responding.** There will be several different exercises for responding to the psalm.

Appendix A

Types of Psalms[56]

Hymns. Hymns are songs of praise to God. Beginning with a "call to worship," the psalmist invites the congregation to lift their praises to the Lord, declares the reasons for that praise—God's mighty acts in the past or his attributes—and concludes with another call for celebration and praise.

Laments. Laments, also called "psalms of complaint," can be either individual laments (focusing on social persecution and illness) or community laments (focusing on national crises). The psalmist begins with (1) an address to God, followed by (2) the complaint in distress, (3) a protest of innocence, (4) a petition for deliverance, and (5) a declaration of confidence in God's character and a vow to praise him.

Thanksgiving Psalms. These psalms are a response to a previous lament. Here the psalmist praises God for answered prayer; he declares that he will praise God (30:1a), summarizes the reason for praise (30:1b–3), recounts the past time of need and his prayer (30:6–10), provides some teaching about God (30:4–5), and declares again his intent (30:12b).

Psalms of Confidence. In such psalms the psalmist expresses his complete confidence in God even in the face of danger, threats, or enemies. These psalms often champion metaphors describing God as a defender and protector (for example, "The Lord *is my shepherd,*" Ps 23:1).

Wisdom Psalms. Wisdom psalms are similar to Proverbs. Their language and style sound a lot like wisdom literature, often setting up a contrast between wise and foolish behavior. Their objective is to instruct.

Psalms of Remembrance. Also known as "storytelling psalms," these focus on God's past acts of redemption.

---

[56]   See LaSor, Hubbard, and Bush, *Old Testament Survey*, 433–440; Anderson, *Out of the Depths*, 235–242; and Longman, *How to Read the Psalms*, 24–36.

Enthronement Psalms. There are eight "enthronement" psalms in the Psalter (Pss 29, 47, 93, 95–99). And although it would be natural to think these have to do with the Davidic kings, in reality they celebrate the *divine* king of Israel and his enthronement over not merely Israel but over all peoples and even the cosmos itself. Their objective is to provoke the people of God to worship Yahweh, "the great God, the great King above all gods!" (Ps 95:3).

Royal Psalms. Royal psalms focus on the Davidic kings and their role in Israel. These psalms celebrate the kings in their coronations (Ps 2), royal weddings (Ps 45), and victories in battle (Ps 20).

Psalms of Ascent. Three times a year all Israel journeyed to Jerusalem for the pilgrim festivals. In these psalms the pilgrims share their expectations as they make their way to Jerusalem to celebrate.

Liturgical Psalms. Much like our liturgies today, the Israelites recited liturgies during specific worship events. They used these liturgical psalms for things such as covenant renewal ceremonies and enthronement ceremonies.

Appendix B

Psalms by Type[57]

Type	Book I 1–41	Book II 42–72	Book III 73–89	Book IV 90–106	Book V 107–150
Hymns	8, 9, 10, 33	46, 48, 66	76, 84, 87	100, 103, 104	111, 113, 114, 117, 145–150
Laments	3, 4, 5, 6, 7, 12, 13, 14, 17, 22, 25, 26, 28, 31, 35, 38, 39, 41	42, 43, 44, 51–61, 64, 69, 70, 71	74, 77, 79, 80, 83, 85, 86, 88	90, 94, 102	109, 137, 139, 140, 141, 142, 143
Thanksgiving Psalms	30, 32, 34, 40	65, 67	75	92	107, 116, 118, 138
Psalms of Confidence	11, 16, 23, 27	62, 63		91	
Wisdom Psalms	1, 19, 37	49	73		112, 119
Psalms of Remembrance			78	105, 106	135, 136
Royal Psalms	2, 18, 20, 21	45, 72	89	101	110, 144
Enthronement Psalms	29	47		93, 95, 96, 97, 98, 99	
Liturgies	15, 24	50, 68	81, 82		115
Psalms of Ascent					120–134

---

[57] Note that some psalms could be placed in more than one of these types. For example, Psalm 18 is a royal psalm and also a thanksgiving psalm.

Bibliography

Anderson, Bernhard. *Out of the Depths*. Philadelphia: Westminster, 1983.

Brueggemann, Walter. "Psalms in Narrative Performance." Pages 9–30 in *Performing the Psalms*. Edited by Dave Bland and David Fleer. St. Louis, MO: Chalice Press, 2005.

Cogan, Mordechai. "Into Exile: From the Assyrian Conquest of Israel to the Fall of Babylon." Pages 242–275 in *The Oxford History of the Biblical World*, ed. Michael D. Coogan. New York: Oxford University Press, 1998.

Cox, Ronald. "The New Testament Preaches the Psalms." Pages 83–104 in *Performing the Psalms*. Edited by Dave Bland and David Fleer. St. Louis: Chalice, 2005.

DeVaux, Roland. *Ancient Israel: Its Life and Institutions*. Grand Rapids: William B. Eerdmans Publishing Co., 1997.

Dumbrell, William. *The Faith of Israel*. Grand Rapids: Baker Academic, 2002.

Faust, Abraham. *Judah in the Neo-Babylonian Period: The Archaeology of Desolation*. Atlanta: Society of Biblical Literature, 2012.

Frankfort, Henri. *Kingship and the Gods: A Study of Ancient Near Eastern Religion as the Integration of Society and Nature*. Chicago: University of Chicago Press, 1978.

Greengus, Samuel. *Laws in the Bible and in Early Rabbinic Collections*. Eugene, OR: Cascade, 2011.

Hilber, John W. *Royal Psalms in Cultic Prophecy in the Psalms*. Berlin: DeGruyter, 2005.

Holladay, William L. *A Concise Hebrew and Aramaic Lexicon of the Old Testament*. Leiden: Brill, 1988.

"It's All About Me." https://tvtropes.org.pmwiki.pmwiki.php/Main/ItsAllAboutMe.

Keil, C. F. and F. Delitzsch. *Commentary on the Old Testament: Psalms*. Vol. 5. Peabody, MA, 1989.

Keller, Phillip. *The Shepherd Trilogy*. Grand Rapids: Zondervan, 1996.

Koehler, Ludwig, Walter Baumgartner, and Johann J. Stamm. *The Hebrew and Aramaic Lexicon of the Old Testament (HALOT)*. Translated and edited under the supervision of Mervyn E. Richardson. 4 vols. Leiden: Brill, 1994–1999.

Kugel, James. *The Idea of Biblical Poetry*. Johns Hopkins University Press, 1981.

"Lament for Ur." https://etcsl.orinst.ox.ac.uk/cgi-bin/etcsl.cgi?text=t.2.2.2&charenc=j# or https://oi.uchicago.edu/sites/oi.uchicago.edu/files/uploads/shared/docs/as12.pdf.

Laniak, Timothy S. *Shepherds After My Own Heart: Pastoral Traditions and Leadership in the Bible.* New Studies in Biblical Theology 20. Downers Grove, IL: InterVarsity Press, 2006.

LaSor, W. S., D. A. Hubbard, and F. W. Bush. *Old Testament Survey: The Message, Form, and Background of the Old Testament* 2nd ed. Grand Rapids: Eerdmans, 1996.

Lewis, C. S. *The Complete Chronicles of Narnia.* Great Britain: HarperCollins, 1998.

Longman III, Tremper. *How to Read the Psalms.* Downer's Grove, IL: InterVarsity, 1988.

Master, Daniel. "Comments on Obed Lipschits." *Journal of Hebrew Scriptures* 7 (2016): 31–32.

Mental-Health-Facts-for-Refugees-1.pdf

Muhlestein, Kerry. "Execration Ritual." *UCLA Encyclopedia of Egyptology,* https://escholarship.org/uc /item/3f6268zf.

Noll, Mark. "We Are What We Sing: Our classic hymns reveal evangelicalism at its best." *Christianity Today* 43.8 (1999): 40.

Olsen, Ted. "Officials Erode Psalm Displays at Grand Canyon." Posted July 1, 2003. *Christianity Today* https://www.christianitytoday.com/ct/2003/julyweb-only/7-14-11.0.html.

Peterson, Andrew. "Is He Worthy?"

"Prayer of Lamentation to Ishtar." http://factsanddetails.com/world/cat56/sub402/entry-6058.html# chapter-21.

Reardon, Patrick. *Christ in the Psalms.* Ben Lomond, CA: Conciliar Press, 2000.

Richter, Sandra L. *Stewards of Eden.* Downer's Grove, IL: InterVarsity Press, 2020.

Richter, Sandra L. "What Do I Know of Holy? On the Person and Work of the Holy Spirit in Scripture." Pages 23–38 in *Spirit of God: Christian Renewal in the Community of Faith.* Edited by Jeffrey W. Barbeau and Beth Felker Jones. Downer's Grove, IL: InterVarsity, 2015.

Save the Children. https://www.savethechildren.org/us/what-we-do/emergency-response/refugee -children-crisis/refugee-stories

Smith, George Adam. *The Historical Geography of the Holy Land.* BiblioLife, LLC, 2009.

Tennent, Julie, ed. *Sing: Singing the Psalms.* Asbury Theological Seminary 2012 Spring Reader.

Terrien, Samuel. *The Psalms and Their Meaning for Today.* Indianapolis: The Bobbs-Merrill Company, Inc., 1952.

Waltke, Bruce K., "Superscripts, Postscripts, or Both." *Journal of Biblical Literature* 110/4 (1991): 583–96.

Wesley, John. "Directions for Singing," Page vii in *The United Methodist Hymnal: Book of United Methodist Worship.* Nashville: The United Methodist Publishing House, 1989.

Westermann, Claus. *The Psalms: Structure, Content & Message.* Minneapolis: Augsburg, 1980.

Wright, Christopher, J. H. *Deuteronomy.* Grand Rapids: Baker, 1996.

About the Author

Dr. Sandra Richter is the Robert H. Gundry Chair of Biblical Studies at Westmont College. She earned her PhD from Harvard University in Hebrew Bible and her MA in Theological Studies from Gordon-Conwell Theological Seminary. She has taught at Asbury Theological Seminary, Wesley Biblical Seminary, and Wheaton College. Because of her passion for the real people and places of the biblical narrative, she has spent many years directing Israel Studies programs that focus on historical geography and field archaeology. Sandy has a heart for the church and bringing high scholarship to the body. She is best known for her book *The Epic of Eden: A Christian Entry into the Old Testament* and its associated Bible studies: Epic of Eden, Isaiah, Jonah, Ruth, and Psalms.

Also Available from Sandra Richter, PhD

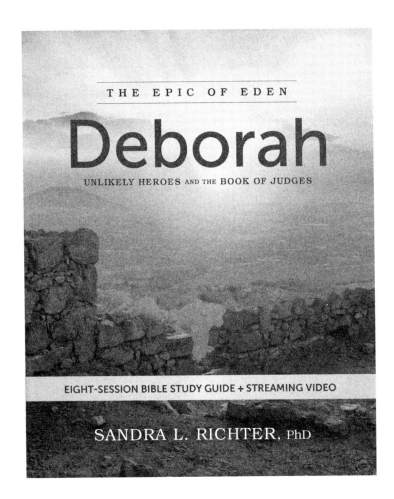

Keep learning with the original Epic of Eden Video Study Series!

Sandra Richter's evocative and compelling *The Epic of Eden* series has helped thousands of churches and individual believers discover the deep beauty of the Old Testament, with the story of Jesus that lies in the heart of it. Legendary Bible stories take on new life as Dr. Richter clearly articulates their part of a larger pattern, revealing an even deeper significance for the stories individually.